The Castles & Bishops Palaces of Pembrokeshire

Monuments in the Landscape

Volume X

The Castles & Bishops Palaces of Pembrokeshire

by
Lise Hull

Logaston Press

LOGASTON PRESS
Little Logaston Woonton Almeley
Herefordshire HR3 6QH

First published by Logaston Press 2005
Copyright © text Lise Hull 2005
Copyright © illustrations Lise Hull 2005, excepting those on
pages 41, 59, 62 (top), 65, 68, 76, 84, 87, 88, 91, 112, 122,
125 (bottom), 154, 155, 156, 161, 162, 185, 193, 205
for which © Logaston Press 2005

ISBN 1 904396 31 3

Set in Times by Logaston Press
and printed in Great Britain by
Hobbs the Printers

Contents

		page
	Author's Introduction	ix
	Acknowledgments	xi
I	The Rise and Fall of the Kingdom of Deheubarth	1
II	Little England Beyond Wales	11
III	The Tudor Transformation	27
IV	Decline and Restoration	35
	Amroth	41
	Angle	43
	Begelly	47
	Benton	48
	Caldey Priory	50
	Camrose	52
	Carew	54
	Carew 'Rectory'	65
	Carswell	66
	Castell Crychydd / Heron's Castle	68
	Castell Fartin / Ma(e)norowen	69
	Castell Llainfawr	69
	Castell Pengawsai / Blaenllechog	70
	Castell Pen Yr Allt	71
	Castell Poeth	72
	Castlebythe	73
	Castlemartin	74
	Castlemorris	75
	Castle Pill	76

Cilgerran	77
Creswell	84
Dale	85
Dingstopple	86
Drim	87
Dyffryn Mawr / Parc y Domen	88
Eastington / Jestynton	89
Eglwyswrw	91
Glyn Patel / Green Castle / Crinow	92
Haroldston	93
Haverfordwest	96
Haycastle	109
Hean / Hen Castell	110
Henry's Moat / Castell Hendre	111
Lampeter Velfrey / Castell Cynon	112
Lamphey Palace	113
Letterston / Parc Moat	120
Llanfrynach	120
Llangwathen	121
Llawhaden	122
Lydstep	128
Maenclochog	131
Manorbier	132
Minwear	141
Narberth	142
Nevern / Nanhyfer	149
Newhouse /Castell Coch	154
New Moat	156
Newport / Trefdraeth	158
Newport (ringwork)	161
Parc y Castell	162
Parc y Marl	163

Paterchurch Tower   164
Pembroke   166
Picton   182
Picton Motte   185
Pointz Castle   187
Puncheston / Castell Moel   188
Roch   189
Rudbaxton   192
Rudbaxton rath / The Rath   193
St Davids Palace   195
St Ishmaels   204
Templeton / Sentence Castle   205
Tenby   207
Upton   214
Walwyn's Castle   216
West Tarr   217
Wiston   218
Wolf's Castle / Cas Blaidd   222

References   223

Please note

Many of the monuments mentioned in this book are situated on private land and permission from the owner must, therefore, be obtained before visiting them.

The following points should also be observed:
1. When visiting sites in the countryside, always follow the Countryside Code.
2. On all sites, extreme care should be taken.
3. Any artefacts found on sites should be reported to the nearest museum.
4. Under no circumstances should visitors dig on or around any site. Any damage could result in prosecution.
5. It is an offence under the 1979 Ancient Monuments and Archaeological Areas Act to use metal detectors on or near scheduled ancient monuments. In addition, simple 'treasure hunting' near ancient monuments can damage evidence to such an extent that archaeologists are unable to interpret it fully in the future.

Author's Introduction

When I first rode BritRail into Haverfordwest on my way to a new military posting at Brawdy, I had no idea that the journey would transform my life. Now, almost 20 years later, I can still vividly remember my first view of the hulking brown ruins that dominate the town centre. As an American, newly arriving in the UK suddenly thrust into the passenger's seat in a car driving on the opposite side of the road to which I was accustomed, I had my hands full clutching the armrest as the person who picked me up at the railway station plummeted towards the overburdened round-about near the river. Yet, immediately before me, I managed to catch my first glimpse of Haverfordwest Castle. The image was, for me, entrancing.

While some of my acquaintances complained that the castle was nothing more than a shell, it was exactly that shell, that pile of masonry remains, which drew me to it. In time, I discovered that castle ruins have a palpable energy which binds us to the past, and to the lives of those who came into contact with them over time. Castles ooze with history, and are physical proof of an individual's existence or an event having occurred long ago. They chronicle history just as manuscripts and other artefacts document the past, but offer more—the physical remains of the past. Even as monuments to warfare and suppression, castles are an essential part of the historical landscape and heritage of Wales.

The native Welsh had little need for heavily fortified private dwellings prior to the arrival of the Normans. Indeed, castles did not appear in south-western Wales until 1093, when the Normans began building an earthwork fortress on a promontory jutting into the Pembroke River. Even then, Welsh leaders continued to occupy large halls, known as *neuaddau*, which were enclosed with weak defences, or no defences at all. In time, they began building castles, as a way to counteract the intrusion of the Normans into Wales and deal with the changing sociopolitical structure the outsiders planted onto the Welsh. Nonetheless, most of Pembrokeshire's castles were erected by the Anglo-Normans and settlers, like the Flemings, who were encouraged to populate the area in the 12th century.

Because so many visitors to Wales scurry to the Edwardian masterpieces in the north, they often fail to realise that West Wales has a plethora of impressive castles, both in ruin and not, both large and small, which impacted upon the course of Welsh, British and world history. Pembrokeshire also hosted some remarkable medieval bishops palaces and a bishop's castle, at Llawhaden. Clearly, the Bishops of St Davids were powerful landowners who carried as much influence in medieval politics as their secular counterparts. For that reason, I have chosen to include several medieval ecclesiastical structures in this book.

Having first discovered Pembrokeshire's castles in the 1980s, I have since made castle research a lifelong pursuit. In the process, I returned to Wales in 1999 to gain a Master's Degree with Distinction in Heritage Studies from the Department of History and Welsh History at the University of Wales Aberystwyth. I have explored well over 300 castles throughout Wales and the British Isles. I have wandered their baileys and clambered up their towers in all kinds of weather, and have found each one distinctive in its own right. This book is a product of my ongoing relationship with Wales, its historic landscape, and with Pembrokeshire in particular.

Lise Hull, 2005

Acknowledgments

The completion of this book would not have been possible without the assistance of the following individuals, who willingly offered their expertise, advice and experiences dealing with the castles and history of Pembrokeshire. I greatly appreciate their taking the time to share their knowledge with me: Michael Freeman, John Kenyon, Neil Ludlow, and Roger Turvey. I would also like to thank Andy Johnson at Logaston Press for enthusiastically supporting this project and for trekking to the sites that I was unable to visit due to other commitments.

My thanks also to Marvin Hull, who accompanied me on much of the journey through Wales and also offered suggestions, memory prompts and another pair of eyes as I waded through this manuscript.

Pembrokeshire has a special place in my heart. I return there frequently, not only to explore its castles, but also to replenish my soul.

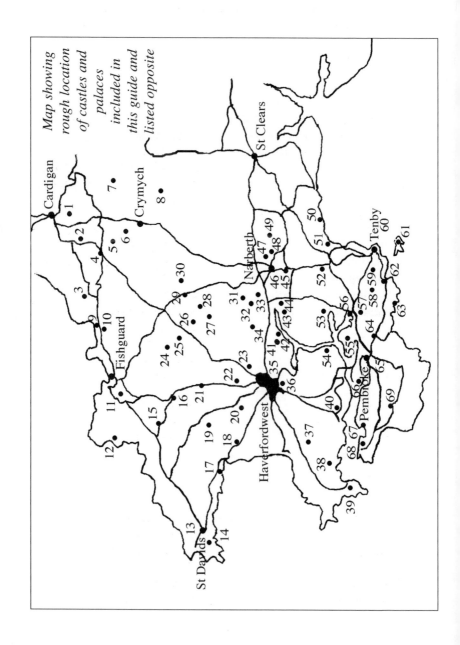

Map showing rough location of castles and palaces included in this guide and listed opposite

Castles and Palaces included in the guide
Numbers relate to the location on the map opposite

1. Cilgerran
2. Castell Pen Yr Allt
3. Nevern / Nanhyfer
4. Eglwyswrw
5. Castell Llainfawr
6. Dyffryn Mawr / Parc y Domen
7. Castell Crychydd / Heron's Castle
8. Llanfrynach
9. Newport (ringwork)
10. Newport
11. Castell Fartin / Ma(e)norowen
12. Castell Poeth
13. St Davids Palace
14. Parc y Castell
15. Castlemorris
16. Letterston
17. Pointz Castle
18. Roch
19. Haycastle
20. Camrose
21. Wolf's Castle
22. Rudbaxton
23. Rudbaxton Rath / The Rath
24. Puncheston
25. Castlebythe
26. Henry's Moat / Castell Hendre
27. Parc y Marl
28. New Moat
29. Maenclochog
30. Castell Pengawsai / Blaenllechog
31. Drim
32. Dingstopple
33. Llawhaden
34. Wiston
35. Haverfordwest
36. Haroldston
37. Walwyn's Castle
38. St Ishmaels
39. Dale
40. Castle Pill
41. Picton
42. Picton Motte
43. Minwear
44. Newhouse / Castell Coch
45. Templeton / Sentence Castle
46. Narberth
47. Llangwathen
48. Glyn Patel / Green Castle / Crinow
49. Lampeter Velfrey / Castell Cynon
50. Amroth
51. Hean / Hen castell
52. Begelly
53. Creswell
54. Benton
55. Upton
56. Carew
57. Carew 'Rectory'
58. West Tarr
59. Carswell
60. Tenby
61. Caldey
62. Lydstep
63. Manorbier
64. Lamphey Palace
65. Pembroke
66. Paterchurch Tower
67. Eastington / Jestynton
68. Angle
69. Castlemartin

I   The Rise and Fall of the Kingdom of Deheubarth

Well before the Normans built their first castle in Pembrokeshire, a hereditary dynasty of native Welsh princes controlled west Wales. Their kingdom, known as Deheubarth, encompassed not only modern Pembrokeshire but spread as far east as the River Towy. Deheubarth was one of three major regions in Wales dominated by major ruling families, the other two being Gwynedd and Powys. Lesser dynasties dominated smaller areas within Wales, including Morgannwg, Brycheiniog, Gwent and Meirionydd. The stability of each territory was precarious at best, despite the hereditary nature of succession within the kingdoms—or perhaps because of. Based on the law of partibility, Welsh inheritance decreed that sons received equal shares of their father's property. Consequently, rivalries and bloodshed were common, as brothers vied with brothers—and princes from other areas—for control.

Medieval Wales in the 11th century was ripe for the picking. Rival dynasties raided each other's territory, seeking more land and power. At times, charismatic leaders, like Hywel Dda and Gruffydd ap Llywelyn, forged a united Wales. But the Wales of the native princes was only sporadically united, politically but not emotionally, and time and again opposing factions resumed their struggle for territorial control. In many ways the law of partibility guided the course of Welsh history, for it weakened Welsh resistance against outside invasion and set the scene for the Norman occupation of much of Wales. That occupation ultimately led to the union of Wales with England, first enacted in the form of the Statute of

Rhuddlan in the 13th century and then solidified by Henry VIII's Acts of Union 300 years later.

In about 905, Cadell ap Rhodri gained control of a large portion of south-western Wales, an area that included both Dyfed and Ystrad Tywi. Together, the two regions became the kingdom of Deheubarth, which Cadell's son, Hywel, inherited upon his father's death five years later. In time, Hywel ap Cadell received the epithet Dda (or 'the Good'), for his keen ability to rule fairly and astutely. Indeed, most historians consider Hywel Dda as the real founder of the kingdom of Deheubarth, which he ruled on his own from 920 after the death of his brother, Clydog, who had shared control with Hywel until that point. Hywel wasted no time in making reconciliation with the Saxons and he frequently visited the court of Aethelstan in Wessex. In time, Hywel Dda fought with the Saxons against his Welsh countrymen in Gwynedd, which he seized in about 942. Hywel became the most powerful king of Wales, a position also claimed by his grandfather, Rhodri Mawr, in the previous century. According to tradition, Hywel's greatest contribution to Welsh history was the codification of Welsh law, sometimes known as 'Cyfraith Hywel', systematising many legal customs which had evolved over time.

After Hywel's death in about 950, the Welsh princes maintained control of their homeland, but sparring between dynasties continued. Almost a century later, Gruffydd ap Llywelyn, a descendant of Hywel Dda, established another uneasy alliance in Wales, taking control by piecemeal conquest. Shortly after seizing Gwynedd in 1039, Gruffydd marched to Deheubarth and finally captured the southern kingdom in about 1056. From then until his death in 1063, Gruffydd ap Llywelyn controlled all of Wales. He also sought an alliance with the Saxons. However, ongoing hostilities both in Wales and England, which Gruffydd periodically attacked, so irritated Edward the Confessor that the Saxon king ordered his minions, led by Harold and Tostig Godwinson, to oust the Welshman from power. By land and by sea, and aided by the Welsh as well, the Saxons tracked Gruffydd into North Wales. In the mountains of Snowdonia, members of Gruffydd's own household murdered their king. Afterwards they allegedly sent his head to the Saxons. Not surprisingly, Wales again split into factions, as the heirs to Deheubarth, Morgannwg, Powys, and Gwynedd staked their hereditary claims. Three years later, in 1066, Edward the Confessor died, Harold Godwinson became King Harold II, and the Saxons were primed for a different fate, which culminated with their king's death at the Battle of Hastings.

Even after Duke William of Normandy conquered the Anglo-Saxons to become King William I, Wales received little attention from the Normans, who were focused on the annexation of England. Deheubarth regained its rightful king, Maredudd ab Owain, and in 1075, Rhys ap Tewdwr, another descendant of Rhodri Mawr and Hywel Dda, became king of Deheubarth. Prior to the death of Rhys ap Tewdwr in 1093, the princes of Deheubarth controlled west Wales and the Normans rarely ventured that far west — William the Conqueror himself apparently only once managed to reach St Davids, meeting with Rhys during what was termed a pilgrimage in 1081. In return, Rhys paid homage to the new king and established a truce of sorts with the Normans. With the exception of occasional raids into west Wales, which increased in frequency when the Conqueror died in 1087, the Normans stayed away from the area until 1093.

Long rivals for control of southern Wales, the kings of Brecheiniog and Deheubarth had clashed several times prior to the arrival of the Normans. Indeed, throughout Rhys ap Tewdwr's reign in Deheubarth, conflicts between rival families plagued Wales. The princes of Powys had challenged his authority and in 1088 forced the Welshman to flee to Ireland. Upon his return, bolstered by an army of Irish and Welsh supporters, Rhys reclaimed his kingdom but could not quell the upheaval.

The Normans began the piecemeal acquisition of southern Wales after the death of William I in 1087 and the coronation of his son, William Rufus, as William II. Like his father, Rufus had ambitious goals for the control of the new Norman kingdom, which not only included the consolidation of the conquest in England but also expansion into Wales.

In late 1088, shortly after a group of Marcher lords failed in their attempt to overthrow the king, one of the rebels, Bernard de Neufmarché, instigated the Norman 'conquest' of south-eastern Wales. Retaining the king's favour, de Neufmarché, a Norman lord who had acquired estates in Herefordshire by right of marriage to the daughter of Osbern FitzRichard, first took Glasbury, where he erected a motte castle on the Welsh side of the border with England and then solidifying his control of the region. For the next five years the Normans progressively extended their grasp on South Wales, constructing a series of earth and timber castles and pushing into Bronllys, towards Usk and finally into Brecon in 1093, where de Neufmarché established a power base, erected a substantial motte castle and also acquired the lordship from his king, William I.

Later that year the native Welsh kings of Brecheiniog and Deheubarth banded together to halt the intrusion of the Normans into their homeland. Marching to Brecheiniog, Rhys ap Tewdwr and Bleddyn ap Maenarch encountered a force of Norman soldiers led by Bernard de Neufmarché not too far from Brecon Castle. During the ensuing struggle the Normans killed Rhys ap Tewdwr. The internecine chaos that followed in the wake of Rhys' death provided the ideal opportunity for the Normans to seize more of southern Wales.

Historical records first document the arrival of the Normans in eastern Glamorgan in 1072, when they supported Prince Caradog ap Gruffydd of Gwynllwg in an affray against Maredudd ab Owain, Prince of Deheubarth. Caradog vigorously supported William I and for almost a decade acted as King of Morgannwg. In 1081, he was killed when battling Rhys ap Tewdwr at Mynydd Carn. After ap Tewdwr's death in 1093, Robert FitzHamon led the Normans against the Welsh and seized lands held by Iestyn ap Gwrgant in Glamorgan. For this, William II created Robert Fitzhamon as the first Lord of Glamorgan. In turn, FitzHamon reputedly granted portions of his newly acquired lordship to 12 of his most devoted followers who established knights' fees centred by castles. Ultimately, it took until the late 13th century for the lords of Glamorgan to solidify their control over the Welsh in South Wales. Administered from Cardiff, the lordship of Glamorgan stretched from the River Rhymney on the east to the River Neath on the west. To the north, the harsh uplands of Blaenau Morgannwg remained largely in Welsh control, whereas the fertile lowlands of Bro Morgannwg were occupied by the Normans.

While Robert FitzHamon consolidated Norman control of Glamorgan, Roger de Montgomery, Earl of Shrewsbury, sent his son, Arnulf, and another contingent of Norman soldiers into Pembrokeshire, then the western part of Dyfed. Like the history of the 'conquest' of Glamorgan, that of Pembrokeshire is not well documented. I.W. Rowlands in volume II of the *Pembrokeshire County History* states with relative certainty that the Normans, commanded by Arnulf de Montgomery, entered Dyfed from the north after marching through Cardigan, and headed towards the site that would become Pembroke Castle.[1] Apparently they met little resistance from the Welsh as they moved southwards through the area, and easily established the lordship of Pembroke.

Almost immediately after Arnulf de Montgomery founded his seat at Pembroke in 1093, the Normans began to anglicise Pembrokeshire. Quite possibly, de Montgomery actually established a 'castellarium' at Pembroke rather than an earldom in the strictest sense of the word. If so, he probably headed a group of dependent military tenancies. In return for the privilege of having their own, albeit lesser, strongholds and estates, his vassals would have provided defensive support (castle-guard) for Pembroke Castle. The castellarium, if Arnulf did indeed impose such a social order upon the region, forced the native Welsh population towards the Preselis.

Yet the Welsh refused to acquiesce in silence. In early 1094 they began a period of rebellion against Norman occupation which lasted four years and saw the destruction of every Norman castle in Dyfed, except for Pembroke and Rhyd-y-Gors (near Carmarthen). The *Brut y Tywysogyon* (*The Chronicle of the Princes*) recorded the highlights of the rebellion which spread across southern Wales as far east as Glamorgan, Brycheiniog and Gwent, and also into northern Wales, where in about 1096 the Earl of Shrewsbury pushed westwards to Anglesey, prompting the Welsh leaders, Cadwgan ap Bleddyn and Gruffydd ap Cynan, to flee to safety in Ireland. The chronicles record that both Welsh and Norman forces ravaged Pembrokeshire as the Welsh continued to fight for their freedom. By this time, however, Pembroke Castle was in the capable hands of constable Gerald de Windsor, who managed to repel the Welsh with deception, even though his garrison was on the verge of starvation (see under the entry for Pembroke Castle).

By 1098, Welsh zeal for the uprising waned. Cadwgan ap Bleddyn and Gruffydd ap Cynan had returned to Wales, made their peace with the Normans and were allowed to control portions of Powys, Ceredigion and Anglesey. The Welsh heirs to Deheubarth, Rhys ap Tewdwr's sons, scattered. Gruffydd fled to safety in Ireland while Hywel suffered imprisonment and mutilation at the hands of the Normans.

For all intents and purposes the Normans now controlled Deheubarth. After the death of their king, William II, and the resulting coronation of Henry I, their attention shifted to the power struggle that erupted between the new king and Robert de Belleme, Earl of Shrewsbury and Arnulf de Montgomery's brother. Despite the losses in west Wales, the Welsh continued to assert their ancestral claims to Deheubarth, and periodically made incursions across southern Wales to threaten the Normans.

The changing landscape
The arrival of the Normans changed the social and political structure of Wales and also drastically altered the Welsh landscape. Pembrokeshire's strategic location, midway between England and Ireland, made it particularly alluring. While the Normans did not conquer Deheubarth *per se*, they ultimately constructed some 55 castles, established new settlements throughout Pembrokeshire and also replaced the Welsh bishop of St Davids with a Norman counterpart, who began a large-scale building programme that resulted in the construction of palaces and a castle for the bishops. The relatively high density of castles in Pembrokeshire reveals much about the Norman psyche—the Welsh must have been intimidating opponents who posed a constant threat to land and livelihood. The power of the threat was proportionate to the number of castles thrown up by the Normans.

The initial burst of castle-building in Pembrokeshire essentially took place from the early to mid-12th century, when most of the region's earthwork fortresses appeared. That many earth and timber sites do not appear in the historical record makes dating difficult. Likewise the fact that, as at Walwyn's Castle, some medieval builders chose to reuse the ramparts and ditches of prehistoric fortifications to enclose their own castles makes the classification of

The motte and ditch at Wiston Castle

many sites (particularly the ringworks) speculative at best. The county's 34 earthwork castles were fairly evenly distributed between mottes (18) and ringworks (16), many of which have yet to be excavated and have been heavily eroded or ploughed.

Motte castles generally consisted of an artificially sculpted, flat-topped mound, packed with earth and often revetted with timber and stone. Rising well above ground level, mottes varied in height from as low as five or six feet to well over 50 feet, the diameters of their summits ranging from 20 feet to 380 feet across. Among the most impressive is Wiston Castle, named for Wizo the Fleming, who probably built the fine motte and bailey in about 1110. Natural hillocks were often reshaped for use as mottes, or labourers piled field stones or earth from what became the enclosing ditch onto the mound to create a usable foundation for timber structures. Most motte castles were supported by at least one large bailey, an ovoid area enclosed by earthen embankments and defended with timber palisades. Construction required little skilled labour, and could proceed relatively quickly and inexpensively. More than likely it took at least several weeks and probably months to excavate and complete a motte and bailey castle.

The typical ringwork castle featured a mound of low to moderate size encircled with ditches and earthen banks, which were topped with timber palisades. The summit was scooped out, so that the outer perimeter stood taller than the centre of the mound. Unlike the motte and bailey castle, fewer ringwork castles acquired substantial stone structures, as occurred at Llawhaden. Pembrokeshire has a notable number of ringwork castles scattered throughout the county but primarily located on the northern side of the Preselis.

Within 50 years of the Norman intrusion into Pembrokeshire, a line of earth and timber castles appeared on the southern side of the inhospitable Preseli hills, creating a barrier that reinforced the physical and political separation of the Welsh from their Anglo-Norman overlords. From west to east these castles include: Castell Mael (Puncheston) at Castlebythe, Henry's Moat (which New Moat later replaced), and Maenclochog, the last of which no longer survives. A second group of earthwork castles, each bearing Welsh names and located in Welsh-speaking areas, delineated the northern side of the Preselis: Pen-yr-Allt, Eglwyswrw, Llainfawr, Llanfyrnach, and Castell Crychydd. D.J. Cathcart King in volume II of the *Pembrokeshire County History* speculates that the builders of the northern cluster of castles, the majority of which appear to have been ringworks, may have been members of the 'uchelwyr', lesser landowners, or Welsh undertenants of lower status than their English counterparts, while Norman vassals of the lords of Cemmaes were responsible for the castles—mainly mottes—along the southern side of the Preselis on lands they received in exchange for 'knight's service'.

In time, the divide between the Welshry and the Englishry acquired the appellation 'landsker line'. The exact origins of the term remain speculative. Some historians believe the word to be Norse and said to mean, simply, a boundary. Others quite plausibly believe the phrase derives from the Anglo-Saxon *landshard* or *landsherd*, words that describe strips of unploughed land acting as boundary markers between two fields or larger parcels of land. In Pembrokeshire, the landsker line does refer to a boundary, but not only does the term relate to a regional division, it also identifies the linguistic and cultural barriers created when the Anglo-

Normans pushed westward after the death of Rhys ap Tewdwr in 1093.

From 1093 onwards, the lives of the native populace in Pembrokeshire were inextricably linked with those of the new settlers. Sometimes intermarriage between the newcomers and native dynasties resulted. At other times rebellion was the response. In the end the Normans interjected a string of stone castles among the earth and timber castles that already stretched from St Davids in the west to Amroth in the east. Together, the strongholds gave the landsker line substance and also visibly defined the divide between the Welshry and English-held Pembrokeshire. The landsker castles broadly included Parc y Castell, Pointz Castle, Hayscastle, Camrose, Rudbaxton, Wiston, Picton motte, Templeton, Glyn Patel, Lampeter Velfrey and Amroth, all of which were earth and timber strongholds, and also the masonry castles at Roch, Haverfordwest, Picton, Llawhaden and Narberth.

In fact, few of Pembrokeshire's earthwork castles developed into substantial masonry fortresses; the majority were either abandoned or later taken over by the Welsh. In many ways formidable Pembroke Castle, which originated as an earth and timber fortress, was an anomaly. Located well south of the landsker line, the castle's strategic riverside location stimulated Pembroke to become the hub of Norman power, the seat of the earldom and also a key administrative and commercial centre.

As the chasm widened between the Welsh and Anglo-Normans, the boundary between the native residents and the occupiers took on not just a physical dimension but had economic and social ramifications as well. The Welsh, now pressed into the fringes of Pembrokeshire, remained dependent on the land and raised livestock in what became known as *pura Wallia*, or pure Wales. The Anglo-Normans, on the other hand, occupied the most fertile regions of south-western Wales, a portion of the *marchia Wallia*— the Welsh Marches—where the lush waterways spawned the growth of several important market towns, each centred by a castle.

As the physical division between the Welshry and Englishry solidified and the Normans drove the Welsh to the farthest reaches of their native kingdom, the region became increasingly anglicised. With the almost simultaneous influx of English, Norman and

Flemish settlers in the early 12th century, Pembrokeshire's demographic makeup also permanently changed, so much so that the region acquired the nickname 'Little England Beyond Wales', which it retains even to this day.

II Little England Beyond Wales

Though no longer ruled by a king after 1093, Deheubarth remained the hereditary kingdom of Rhys ap Tewdwr's descendants—at least in their eyes. Eager to reassert their dynastic dominance, the native princes and their countrymen frequently joined together against the Anglo-Norman occupiers, torching their castles and razing their towns, but never fully regaining control of their ancestral lands. Despite Welsh efforts to the contrary, the Normans established a formidable barrier reinforced by the placement of their castles and pushed the native princes northwards towards the fringes of Deheubarth.

Plunging himself into the politics of the times, Arnulf de Montgomery sided with his brother, Robert de Belleme, the 3rd Earl of Shrewsbury, and the princes of Powys in a rebellion against Henry I in 1101. Supporting Robert of Normandy's claim to the English throne, the rebels accompanied the duke during his invasion of England, when he attempted to seize the monarchy as William II's rightful heir. The failed rebellion led to the signing of the Treaty of Alton, in which Duke Robert acknowledged Henry I as England's king. When Belleme refused to respond to the 45 counts of treason and other charges, Henry captured the rebel's castles at Arundel, Tickhill, Bridgnorth, and Shrewsbury, and forced Belleme into exile in Normandy. Henry I attainted Belleme's brother, Arnulf de Montgomery, for his part in the rebellion, and banished him from the kingdom. Consequently, the lordship and castle of Pembroke became royal property and remained so until

1138, when Stephen became king of England and appointed Gilbert FitzGilbert de Clare as earl of Pembroke.

During the 36 years that Henry I controlled Pembrokeshire, he transformed the region into a heavily anglicised, Anglo-Norman colony. He appointed his own men to govern the lordship of Pembroke and replaced Sulien, the Welsh bishop of St Davids, with his own man, Bernard, in 1115. Most importantly, Henry also encouraged settlers from Devon and Somerset to move into the area and promoted the plantation of groups of Flemings, immigrants from Flanders (now in Belgium), into the cantrefs of Rhos and Daugleddau. Flemish leaders erected castles, founded communities and bequeathed their names to places like Wiston (Wizo's town), Tancredston (Tancred's town) and Letterston (Letard's town). By the beginning of the 13th century the fully anglicised Flemings provided a buffer zone between the caput at Pembroke and the Welsh. The migration of settlers from outside of Wales firmly entrenched the Normans and their vassals as the overlords of 'Little England Beyond Wales'.

Undaunted, the Welsh continued their struggle for power, fighting not just the Normans but their own countrymen as well. In 1113, Rhys ap Tewdwr's disenfranchised son, Gruffydd, returned from Ireland to claim his rightful inheritance. Initially rebuffed by Gruffydd ap Cynan, Prince of Gwynedd, whose support he had sought, the prince of Deheubarth then turned to the younger generation of the local nobility for aid in storming Norman castles and raiding settlements throughout West Wales. In fact, the prince of Gwynedd had already agreed to capture and turn over Gruffydd ap Rhys to the Normans, whose bribes and political favour he sought. However, forewarned of the plot against him, Gruffydd ap Rhys managed to flee to safety and continued his rebellion.

According to the *Brut y Tywysogyon* (*The Chronicle of the Princes*), even though Gruffydd ap Rhys ultimately failed to reclaim his full inheritance, the kingdom of Deheubarth, he managed to make noteworthy gains against the Henry I's army in 1115 and 1116. He swept across southern Wales, attacked Llandovery and Swansea, torched Carmarthen and destroyed the castle of Arberth, probably Sentence Castle. Agreeing to terms with Henry I, Gruffydd managed to regain control of Cantref

Mawr, a small portion of Ceredigion in north-eastern Deheubarth, but little else.

Keeping a low profile in Wales until after the king's death in 1135, when civil war erupted in England, Gruffydd ap Rhys joined his fellow Welshmen, including the sons of Gruffydd ap Cynan, in another revolt against the Normans in Ceredigion and Carmarthen. During the rebellion, which began in the spring of 1136, they defeated a force of Anglo-Normans and Flemings at Crug Mawr, just north of Cardigan, and seized the Norman castle as well. After Gruffydd's death in 1137, his sons successfully destroyed several castles in Ceredigion and also the formidable stronghold at Carmarthen. In response to the destruction, the Normans began replacing their castles' timber defences, which were prone to rot and vulnerable to burning, with stone. They built simple stone gatehouses at Manorbier and Carew castles and gave Haverfordwest Castle a rudimentary stone keep. They also rebuilt domestic buildings in stone, such as Manorbier's great hall block, which probably functioned as a hall-keep and the main focal point of the castle, and Pembroke Castle's first masonry structure, the 'Old Hall', which served a residential rather than defensive role.

Farther afield, a ruined shell keep crowned the summit of the substantial mound at Wiston, the finest of Pembrokeshire's motte castles. At Nevern, not only were two mottes added to the large ringwork castle in the late 12th century, but both also received stonework structures: the Norman-built mound facing north-west probably bore a shell keep; Rhys ap Gruffydd and his sons probably added several masonry structures and a stone revetment onto the summit of the motte on the opposite side of the castle after they ousted the FitzMartins. Fragments of masonry also survive at many smaller earthwork castles, including Eglwyswrw, Castell Crychydd and Castell Pen Yr Allt, but the remains are difficult to characterise.

Unable to simultaneously concentrate on keeping the English throne and quell the rebellion fomenting in west Wales, the new king, Stephen, appointed Gilbert FitzGilbert de Clare as Earl of Pembroke in 1138 to handle the princes of Deheubarth. In 1155, Maredudd ap Gruffydd, by then lord of Ceredigion, Ystrad Tywi and Dyfed, died, leaving his brother, Rhys, the youngest prince of

Deheubarth, to inherit the lordship and to also join with Owain ap Gruffydd ap Cynan (better known as Owain Gwynedd) to oust the unwelcome Anglo-Norman overlords from Wales.

In his youth, Rhys ap Gruffydd had fought alongside his older brothers as they endeavoured to recover their homeland from the Anglo-Normans during the reign of King Stephen. For almost two decades he continued to support his brothers, capturing and destroying of a chain of castles, including Wiston and Tenby. He also fought against countrymen from Gwynedd to retain control of Ceredigion. Consequently Rhys became a formidable warrior, but he also gained crucial skills which transformed him into a shrewd leader who capably sparred with King Henry II, his heirs and vassals in Wales for four decades. Upon Maredudd's death in 1155, much of Wales became a battleground as Rhys initiated an era of uneasy coexistence with the English outsiders and likewise with the native princes of Wales. In time, Rhys ap Gruffydd would become the most powerful of all native Welsh princes and would also re-establish the kingdom of Deheubarth. He is better known as the Lord Rhys.

Even though Henry II gained the acquiescence of most of the native princes, including the powerful Owain Gwynedd, Rhys ap Gruffydd vacillated between superficial submission and open resistance. In the spring of 1158 several Welsh leaders encouraged the Lord Rhys to meet with the English king. In a politically correct but unsettling gesture, Rhys relinquished almost the entirety of Deheubarth. Like his father before him, he only retained control over Cantref Mawr in the remote north-eastern corner of the former kingdom and a few minor spreads of land not valued by the king.

Believing the Welsh problem to be resolved, Henry II embarked on a campaign against the French later that year. After suffering several deaths at the hands of the Normans, led by Walter de Clifford, and enduring the king's failure to come to his aid, the Lord Rhys launched an incursion into west Wales in 1159. According to the *Brut y Tywysogyon*, he destroyed the castles of Dyfed before marching east to besiege Carmarthen Castle. When a contingent of the king's soldiers bolstered by Welshmen from Gwynedd confronted Rhys, he retreated to Cantref Mawr. Rather than surrendering to the English, Rhys accepted a truce.

For the next three years, the Lord Rhys maintained a peace of sorts with the king, but, in 1162, he attacked Cantref Bychan and seized Llandovery Castle, which Walter de Clifford owned. His actions prompted the king's return from France to attack southern Wales himself in 1163. This time Rhys recognised the folly of fighting the stronger English army, and surrendered.

In July 1163, after paying homage to Henry II at Woodstock, Rhys ap Gruffydd returned to his power base at Cantref Mawr. From there he began a new round of assaults against the English in Ceredigion. After allegedly slaughtering the Flemings and burning the countryside, Rhys claimed Ceredigion for the Welsh. In 1165, when inclement weather fortuitously drove the king's army out of Wales, Rhys torched Cardigan and shortly thereafter seized Cilgerran Castle. The *Brut* records that the Normans and Flemings then stormed Cilgerran Castle on two occasions, but suffered significant losses at the hands of the Welsh and were forced to retreat back to Pembroke.

By 1167 the Lord Rhys controlled Ceredigion, Ystrad Tywi and a portion of Dyfed. The following year he expanded into Powys and, with the aid of Owain Gwynedd who had also turned against the king, the Welsh destroyed Rhuddlan and Builth castles. When Owain Gwynedd's death in 1170 thrust northern Wales into dynastic chaos, Rhys seized the day and effectively took control of Welsh Wales.

Meanwhile, in Pembrokeshire, a new Norman invasion was in the offing, this time involving Ireland where the king of Leinster, Dermot (Diarmaid) McMourrough, had contested the position of Rory O'Connor as high-king and fled into exile. Having supported Henry II's aborted assault against the Welsh in 1165, Dermot now turned to England for assistance. Enlisting recruits from Pembrokeshire, including one of the sons of the Lord Rhys, and from other parts of the realm, Dermot attacked the high-king. During the fray, Rhys' son died. Even though O'Connor's men easily defeated their foe, the Irish high-king allowed Dermot to retain the kingdom of Leinster.

Dermot was again soon appealing to England for help against Rory O'Connor. Gathering soldiers from Pembrokeshire, Richard de Clare, the Earl of Pembroke and nicknamed 'Strongbow', staged his successful invasion of Ireland from Pembroke Castle, his king,

Henry II, otherwise occupied in France. Upon Dermot McMourrough's death in 1171, Strongbow acquired the kingdom of Leinster and spent the remainder of his life in Ireland, essentially abandoning the earldom of Pembroke.

By September 1171 Rhys ap Gruffydd had essentially completed the consolidation of Wales, defeating his last Welsh rival, Owain Cyfeiliog. He then met Henry II at Newnham, in the Forest of Dean, where he affirmed his allegiance to England. At the time Henry was preparing his own invasion of Ireland, largely to restrain Strongbow who the king now believed to be a great threat. About ten days later the king and the Lord Rhys again met, this time at Pembroke, where Henry granted the Welsh leader what amounted to complete control of the former kingdom of Deheubarth and also appointed him as justiciar in southern Wales. No Welshman had previously achieved such an honour.

As justiciar Rhys acted on behalf of the king and accordingly levied royal authority over the Welsh leaders in Glamorgan, Gwent and the border with England. How much control he had over the Norman lords is uncertain; however, the earldom of Pembroke did revert to the Crown. Nonetheless, the Lord Rhys had now regained his rightful inheritance and also gained power over the other native princes and lords in the south. He also supplied the king with 300 horses, 4,000 head of cattle and 24 hostages, to demonstrate good faith.[1] The following month, *en route* to battle in Ireland, Henry II again stopped at Pembroke where he confirmed upon Rhys the lands of Ceredigion, Ystrad Tywi, Ystlwyf and Efelffre, which Rhys had secured in 1167.[2] The Welshman remained such a staunch supporter of Henry's that, during the barons' rebellion of 1173, he led a group of his countrymen into England to fight alongside the king.

Besides being a skilled leader who solidified his power with several strategically arranged marriages, the Lord Rhys was a capable warrior who used castles to fortify his grip on southern Wales. During the last two decades of the 12th century he instigated a major castle-building programme at Cardigan, Cilgerran, Dinefwr, Llandovery, Rhyader, Ystrad Meurig, and Nevern. Nevern Castle would play a critical role during the last decade of Rhys' life, when his own sons (eight of whom were legitimate) greedily fought each other—and their father—for power.

After Richard I's accession in 1189, Rhys ap Gruffydd apparently believed his relationship with the monarchy had drastically degraded and initiated several attacks against Anglo-Norman lordships in south and west Wales. He stormed the towns of Haverfordwest and Pembroke, the Gower peninsula and portions of Carmarthen, and seized St Clears, Laugharne and Llansteffan castles. In July, during the siege of Carmarthen Castle, Rhys received a visit from Gerald of Wales, his kinsman, who carried a letter from Richard soliciting his presence to discuss peace terms. Brazenly refusing the king's request, Rhys resumed his assault on the castle, confident that he was making the correct decision. Two months later, Prince John persuaded the Welsh leader, still in the midst of besieging Carmarthen, to meet the king at Oxford. This time, Richard I refused the meeting and angered the Lord Rhys, who swiftly resumed his assault on Carmarthen Castle.

Not only was Rhys at loggerheads with the new king of England, but he also found himself fighting his headstrong sons, primarily Gruffydd and Maelgwyn, for control of Deheubarth. Their rivalry was so strong that, in 1189, Gruffydd, Rhys' eldest son, reputedly managed to persuade his father to imprison Maelgwyn, touted in the *Brut y Tywysogyon* as 'the light and splendour and excellence and the shield and bulwark of all Deheubarth and its liberty, the dread of the Saxons, the best knight, a second Gawain'. Gruffydd then agreed to convey Maelgwyn to the Norman lord, William de Braose. In return, de Braose promised his daughter, Matilda, to Gruffydd in marriage.

In 1191, again at Gruffydd's urging, the Lord Rhys stormed Nevern Castle and evicted the FitzMartins, even though they were kinsmen by marriage. During the following year, Rhys insisted that Gruffydd turn over control of the castle to Maelgwn, after he regained his freedom from de Braose (the *Brut* states that Maelgwn actually escaped). Also in 1192, Rhys seized Llawhaden Castle from the bishops of St Davids and granted southern Dyfed to his son, Hywel Sais. The seemingly generous acts further embittered Rhys' eldest son who considered himself the only rightful heir, regardless of the implications of the law of partibility. By 1193 the conflict between Rhys and his sons ignited into full fledged war, which pitted brother against brother and sons against father.

The sons of the Lord Rhys took their aggression out on several castles, including Ystrad Meurig and Llawhaden, which Maelgwn assaulted, while Hywel Sais stormed Wiston Castle and captured the lord, Philip FitzWizo and his family. In 1194 Hywel Sais turned against his father, and with his brother, Maelgwn, captured and imprisoned the Lord Rhys in Nevern Castle. Hywel soon had a change of heart and released his father, who took control of the castle. During 1195 two other sons, Rhys Gryg and Maredudd, seized Dinefwr Castle and the castle of Cantref Bychan, but their father captured and imprisoned them at Ystrad Meurig Castle in Ceredigion. In 1196 Rhys found himself embroiled in battle against the king's troops and captured several castles in the process, including Painscastle and Carmarthen Castle, which he burned.

In April 1197, Rhys ap Gruffydd, lauded in the *Brut y Tywysogyon* as 'a second Achilles in the sturdiness of his breast, the gentleness of Nestor, the doughtiness of Tydeus, the strength of Samson, the valour of Hector, the fleetness of Eurialius, the comeliness and face of Paris, the eloquence of Ulysses, the wisdom of Solomon, the majesty of Ajax', died from an unknown but reputedly virulent disease (possibly the plague), leaving his sons to their feud and paving the way for the princes of Gwynedd to unify Wales for the final time. Gruffydd ap Rhys donned his father's mantle, but continued to fight his brother, Maelgwn, for power in Deheubarth. Gruffydd's death in 1201 did little to ease the struggle for Deheubarth, and Maelgwn, Hywel Sais and Rhys Ieuanc, Gruffydd's son, continued to vie with each other and with other Welshmen for power. The struggle largely continued outside of Pembrokeshire, and, therefore, is beyond the scope of this book.

During the 13th century, the bishops of St Davids and their secular counterparts embarked upon large-scale building programmes. The bishops began transforming the large ringwork castle at Llawhaden into a masonry stronghold that rivalled all but the most formidable of the secular castles in Pembrokeshire. They also remodelled their residences at St Davids and Lamphey, adding masonry battlements, plain gatehouses and more lavish structures. Even in ruin, the palaces reflect their owners' medieval wealth and status.

Arguably the most important castle-builders in Pembrokeshire were the Earls of Pembroke, who promoted the full-scale change from timber fortifications to heavy stone defences and created the county's most formidable fortresses. William Marshal (the Elder) married Isabel de Clare and was created Earl of Pembroke by King John in 1199. Various commitments, not least service in France, kept Marshal away from Pembroke for five years. Then he instigated a revolution, not just by retaking castles seized by the native Welsh princes after the death of the Lord Rhys, but also by introducing a new architectural feature: Pembroke Castle's great round tower. In time, round towers appeared at other Marshal castles including formidable Chepstow, in south-eastern Wales. Indeed, the design of the Marshal castle at Cilgerran actually mirrored the plan of its grander model at Pembroke.

Early in the 13th century the Welsh renewed their rebellion against King John and the Anglo-Normans in Pembrokeshire, who responded by constructing massive round towers and substantial curtain walls at Manorbier, Carew and Llawhaden castles. However, the native princes also resumed their power struggles with each other. Out of the chaos, Llywelyn ab Iorwerth, Prince of Gwynedd, increasingly assumed control of Wales by forming alliances with the leading Welsh princes, including Maelgwn and Rhys Fychan, two sons of the Lord Rhys. In 1212 the Welsh began their rebellion anew and besieged several castles in northern Wales. They soon agreed, however, to the pope's requests to make peace with the king.

In 1215 England's leading barons rebelled against King John, sparking a protracted civil war that would end for the English with the signing of the Magna Carta but would persist in Wales for much longer. As Llywelyn ab Iorwerth stormed the Welsh Marches, Maelgwn ap Rhys and his nephew, Rhys Ieuanc, banded together for an onslaught on Dyfed, where they devastated Narberth and Maenclochog castles, both of which still featured timber defences. Now firmly numbering the princes of Deheubarth amongst his supporters, Llywelyn razed the castles at Carmarthen, Llansteffan, St Clears and Laugharne. The Welsh rebels then moved westward, seized Newcastle Emlyn castle and devastated Newport and Cilgerran castles. Afterwards, Llywelyn ab Iorwerth allocated the lands they had taken, granting portions of Pembrokeshire, including Cemmaes and Cilgerran Castle, to Maelgwn ap Rhys. The other heirs to the House of Deheubarth received lands and castles in Ceredigion and Ystrad Tywi.

Five years later Llywelyn ab Iorwerth led the Welsh into yet another rebellion in southern Wales, this time targeting the Flemings in Pembrokeshire in retaliation for their assaults on local Welsh residents. The rebels destroyed Wiston Castle and the neighbouring town and also burned the town of Haverfordwest, up to the castle's foundations. According to the *Brut y Tywysogyon*, they also slaughtered many Flemish settlers in the region.

In 1223 the Earl of Pembroke, William Marshal the Younger, finally managed to regain control of Cilgerran and expanded his hold over west Wales to include the old kingdom of Dyfed and the lordships of St Clears and Emlyn. Gathering an army from Ireland, the earl's forces then landed in Pembrokeshire and swiftly moved into Cardigan, Carmarthen and Cilgerran, where Marshal wrested the castles from the Welsh, and secured and repaired them for his own use. The rebels were forced to retreat to the Marches.

By the time Llywelyn ap Gruffydd reignited his grandfather's campaign against English rule in the 1250s, the earldom of Pembroke had passed to William de Valence. In late 1256 Llywelyn and his Welsh supporters began their push southwards towards Pembroke. However, substantial stone fortifications now stood at Narberth, Newport, Carew, Haverfordwest, Picton and Llawhaden, and fortified towers centred Roch, Benton and Upton. The Anglo-Normans had temporarily barred Welsh movement into the region. In 1257, however, Maredudd ap Rhys and Maredudd ab Owain led the rebels in attacks against several castles, including Narberth and Newport, which they briefly seized. They also ravaged the lordship of Haverfordwest but could not take the castle. During the ensuing counteroffensive, the English managed to retake Narberth Castle but not the lordship of Cemmaes.

In 1258 dissatisfaction with Henry III sparked a widespread rebellion by his leading barons, including Simon de Montfort, Earl of Leicester and the king's brother-in-law, and Gilbert de Clare, Earl of Gloucester and Lord of Glamorgan. Accused of mismanaging the realm's finances, the king resisted barons' efforts to supervise his spending habits and refused to agree to the Provisions of Oxford, which curbed his power and formed a truce with the

Welsh. Enraged by the king's defiance, de Montfort led a seven year rebellion against the monarchy. William de Valence, Earl of Pembroke, vigorously supported the king, who was also his half-brother, reputedly believing that the barons had formed an unreasonable alliance with the Welsh. When the barons offered de Valence, his brother Aymer, and Henry's other representatives the choice of unopposed flight to France or custody and execution in England, the king's supporters fled to safety in France.

With the barons' rebellion dominating the king's time and attention, the Welsh shrewdly turned their sights on regaining control of their homeland. A truce was promptly overturned in September of 1258 when the Welsh battled the English near Cilgerran. Even though they renewed the truce in 1259, the English rejected the terms proposed by Llywelyn ap Gruffydd and set the stage for further strife. In 1260, while Henry III was away in France, Maredudd ab Owain attacked and burned the town of Tenby, but was unable to seize the castle. The revolt was followed by yet another truce and two years of calm. William de Valence returned from exile in 1261 and spent the next three years acting as his half-brother's emissary, but fled once again when the conflict between the king and his barons erupted in earnest at Lewes, in southern England, in 1264.

At Lewes, the rebel barons defeated the royalist army and imprisoned the king and his son, Prince Edward, at the castle. Simon de Montfort took control of the government and established what became the model for the British Parliament. However, Edward soon escaped and gathered his own army to confront de Montfort. In 1265 he persuaded Gilbert de Clare to fight for the king at Evesham. During the battle, which took place in August, de Montfort was killed. His death, however, did not end the rebellion, and the garrison at Kenilworth Castle remained loyal to the memory of the Earl of Leicester and his son, another Simon.

Having returned from self-imposed exile in May, William de Valence, Earl of Pembroke, landed in Pembrokeshire and marched with a small contingent of supporters to Haverfordwest, where they seized the castle before joining Prince Edward and Gilbert de Clare during the siege of Gloucester. In 1266 Henry III led royalist troops against de Montfort's men at Kenilworth and effectively suppressed the rebellion. De Valence reacquired control of Pembroke Castle and also become the custodian of Haverfordwest Castle.

In 1267 Henry III signed the Treaty of Montgomery, which officially recognised Llywelyn ap Gruffydd as the Prince of Wales, much to the chagrin of his son and heir, the future King Edward I. The English retained control of Cardigan, Cilgerran and Carmarthen Castles and also held the lordships of Wales that extended from Cemmaes eastward to the Marches. William de Valence spent the remainder of his career serving alongside his nephew, Edward, who became king in 1272 and staged two historic campaigns against the Wales, the first in 1277 and the second in 1282.

During Edward I's second campaign William de Valence, as captain of the army of west Wales, formed an alliance with Rhys ap Maredudd, of the House of Deheubarth, to fight Llywelyn ap Gruffydd. By early 1283 the Welsh war for independence was all but over. The English had killed Llywelyn the previous December, de Valence had gained control of Ceredigion, and Edward I had condemned Dafydd ap Gruffydd, Llywelyn's brother, to death. As in 1277, when England defeated the Welsh during what is known as the first war for independence, the king again believed he had finally conquered the Welsh in 1283.

However, it took only four years for Rhys ap Maredudd to incite an ill-advised rebellion against Robert Tybetot, the king's justiciar in west Wales. The English defeated the rebels and forced Rhys to forfeit his lands. Three years later, Rhys again rebelled; however, this time, he was captured. His execution effectively tolled the death knell for the kingdom of Deheubarth. The native Welsh found themselves on the periphery of their hereditary homeland, subject to the impulses of the Earls of Pembroke and other overlords.

In addition to planting the Flemings and encouraging settlement from England and Flanders, the Anglo-Normans also invited several monastic communities to establish themselves in Wales. In about 1200, Augustinian monks settled on the outskirts of Haverfordwest, then emerging as a major port and commercial centre, and built their monastery on a flat, marshy sweep of land donated by Robert FitzRichard (also known as Robert de Hwlfordd). During the three and a half centuries that Haverfordwest Priory ministered to the needs of the burgeoning town, the monastery became a powerful force and significant landowner in the region. Besides the priory church, the Augustinians acquired control of Haverfordwest's three parish churches and also the smaller churches at Camrose, Llanstadwell, St Ishmaels, Dale and Haroldston St Issells, from which they collected a regular income.

Dominican Black Friars established themselves in Haverfordwest about 50 years after the Augustinian Black Canons. Their main roles within the town would have been to teach their religion and to educate the locals. Unlike the Augustinians, the friars advocated a vow of poverty and depended on donations and bequests to survive. One of their earliest benefactors was King Henry III. Queen Eleanor of Castile also donated money to the friary, while other patrons presented the monks with land-holdings. Sadly, the friary now only survives in local placenames and in the form of a blue plaque; however, the priory has been extensively excavated and consolidated. Managed by Cadw, the public has access throughout the year.

Other ecclesiastical communities were established at Milford Haven, where the Tironensians founded Pill Priory; at Pembroke, where the Benedictines at Monkton Priory provided important support to the neighbouring castle; and at Slebech, where the Hospitallers established the commandery of the Knights of St John of Jerusalem, the only commandery of the order to locate its headquarters in Wales. Anglo-Norman and Flemish lords donated several Pembrokeshire properties to the Hospitallers, including the chapel of St Leonard at Rudbaxton Rath and holdings in Letterston, Amroth, Wiston and Rosemarket. The Knights Templar may have founded a settlement at the village of Templeton, but nothing remains except the placename to give substance to this notion.

The bishops of St Davids were by far the most powerful and prosperous ecclesiastical lords in Pembrokeshire. As Marcher lords they held their lordship at the pleasure of the king, to whom they paid homage. The see of St Davids was the largest diocese in medieval Wales, and the king imbued the bishops with the legal authority to hold courts, fill prisons and maintain a gallows. As mobile bishops, they maintained residences and facilities throughout south-western Wales, including Llawhaden, where they located their administrative centre at the barony's castle, and Lamphey, a manorial centre with its own palace. They had smaller residences at New Moat, Wolf's Castle, Trefin, Warren (on the Castlemartin Peninsula), Llandygwydd, and Llanddewi (on the Gower Peninsula), and also owned 'inns', or great houses, in London and Ludlow. The bishops' most impressive residence—the palace at St Davids—was located in Dewisland, the Welsh cantref of Pebidiog, which Rhys ap Tewdwr probably donated to them.

Several bishops maintained close familial ties with Pembrokeshire's secular lords, including David FitzGerald, the uncle of Gerald of Wales, whose family owned Manorbier Castle, and Gerald himself. It is not surprising that Gerald's lifelong dream was to become Bishop of St Davids. Ironically, even though he achieved fame as an influential cleric, world traveller and renowned chronicler, Gerald the Welshman (*Giraldus Cambrensis*) never fulfilled his greatest ambition—he held the bishopric at Brecon, but not the greater prize, St Davids.

The 14th and 15th centuries in Little England Beyond Wales found both secular and ecclesiastical lords funnelling their finances into new accommodation, ostentation and stylistic conversions, while still maintaining the military integrity of their strongholds. Now, tower houses and other modestly fortified dwellings —many of which were residences of the upwardly mobile gentry class—began to appear in the region. The rectangular tower house at Angle, on the Castlemartin Peninsula, is the best surviving example of its kind in Wales. Built by the Shirburns in the late 14th century possibly to withstand pirate raids, the tower

The tower at Angle

may have seen action in 1405, when Owain Glyndwr's French supporters landed nearby on the shores of Milford Haven. Other examples can be seen at Carswell, Eastington, Haroldston, Lydstep, West Tarr, on Caldey Island, and at Carew. From 1401 to 1405, Owain Glyndwr's men had periodically charged into Pembrokeshire, but they never completely gained control of west Wales. In fact, if anonymous medieval chronicles are accurate, Pembrokeshire may have been an early target of Glyndwr's. In the late spring of 1401, having only managed weak successes in his campaign against English rule in northern Wales, the controversial freedom fighter and his small group of followers turned their attention towards Pembrokeshire, then under the control of Sir William Beauchamp, whom Henry IV named as justiciar of South Wales. Beauchamp gathered an army of some 1,500 men, most of whom came from Pembrokeshire, and advanced northwards to meet Glyndwr at Hyddgen, north of Plynlimon, Ceredigion, where they suffered 200 casualties and a resounding defeat at the hands of the Welsh rebels. The king promptly relieved Sir William of his duties but allowed him to retain the earldom of Pembroke, and appointed Sir Thomas Percy, Earl of Worcester and lord of Haverfordwest and Emlyn, in his stead.

During 1402 and early 1403, as the Glyndwr rebellion spread to other parts of Wales and the rebels made significant gains against the English in Brecon, Glamorgan and Gwent,[3] Thomas Percy began restocking, repairing and garrisoning the castles of Pembrokeshire in anticipation of another Welsh onslaught. By the summer of 1403 many long-time supporters of the king in Pembrokeshire, including David Perrot (the treasurer-chancellor for Pembrokeshire) and Sir Thomas Percy himself, switched their allegiances to Glyndwr. Edmund Mortimer of Narberth Castle had also joined the Welshman's cause. Perrot reputedly helped organise the Welsh naval strategy against the English and may have participated in Glyndwr's victories at Criccieth, Aberystwyth and Harlech castles.

By July, Glyndwr's army had made substantial gains in southern Wales, besieging and seizing several castles, including Dryslwyn, Newcastle Emlyn, Llansteffan and Carmarthen. Nonetheless, a contingent of about 700 Welsh fighters unexpectedly found their way blocked by Sir Thomas Carew, constable of Narberth Castle. Carew's soldiers defeated the rebels before they reached Pembrokeshire. Henry IV then ordered his men to strengthen the castles at Llawhaden, Laugharne, Manorbier, Llandovery and probably Newport and to bolster the garrisons already on station at Haverfordwest, Pembroke, Cilgerran, Narberth and Tenby. Besides granting additional lands and the castle at St Clears to Sir Thomas Carew, the king also placed Sir Francis de Court as lord of Pembroke, presented the lordship of Haverfordwest to his son, the Prince of Wales, and promoted an attitude of resistance against the Welsh. The Welsh in return had recruited aid from the French in the form of a small naval fleet.

As Glyndwr's army moved southwards in 1404, the royalist garrisons at Pembroke, Manorbier and Llawhaden restocked their castles with foodstuffs and other essential items. The rebels devastated the lordship of Roch in November and initiated sieges at Haverfordwest and Tenby, which they evidently abandoned when Christmas approached. The lull in the action lasted until June of 1405, when Owain Glyndwr again marched south, taking Cardigan Castle on his way into Pembrokeshire.

By now scores of local residents had evacuated Pembrokeshire, leaving Little England Beyond Wales especially vulnerable to invasion. In August, some 2,600 Frenchmen landed near Milford Haven and made their way to Haverfordwest to meet with Glyndwr, who had amassed an army of about 10,000 fighters. The rebels sacked Haverfordwest, destroying the mills and ravaging the countryside, but did not take the castle. Then, as the French sailed their ships eastwards from the Haven, the rest of Glyndwr's men marched to Tenby, where they besieged the town. The rebels fled when the English army appeared, but not before putting their ships to the torch to prevent enemy seizure. The freedom fighters moved onwards, heading to Carmarthen where they captured both castle and town, and then marching into battle near Worcester. In November 1405, against the king's express orders, Sir Francis de Court organised a commission to pay the Welsh a ransom of £200 in exchange for a six-month truce. By the middle of 1406 the rebels moved their fight elsewhere in Wales, and the French abandoned Glyndwr's cause, sailing back to France.

III The Tudor Transformation

Almost five centuries after Rhys ap Tewdwr's death, Harri Tudur took his place in the annals of Welsh history by defeating Richard III at the Battle of Bosworth. Born in Pembroke Castle but forced to flee to France for survival, the future king finally began his journey to England after landing on the western coast of Pembrokeshire, at Dale, near what is now Milford Haven. The Welshman's victory over the House of York in 1485 led to his coronation as King Henry VII, the inauguration of the Tudor Dynasty, and the union of Wales and England in 1536.

While mighty Pembroke Castle was the birthplace of the future king, the family also owned a fine estate called Plas Penmynydd on the Isle of Anglesey. Variously spelled Tudur, Tewdwr and Tudor (the anglicised version), the surname means 'territorial king' or 'sir' and actually derives from Tudur ap Goronwy, great-great grandson of Ednyfed Fychan, who was lord steward to Llywelyn ab Iorwerth in the 13th century. During the Owain Glyndwr rebellion in the early 15th century, the Tudurs supported the Welsh freedom fighter against King Henry IV, losing their lands at Penmynydd after Rhys ap Tudur lost his life.

It was not until the rise of Owain ap Maredudd ap Tudur that the spelling, Tudor, was formally adopted and passed to subsequent generations.(Many historians continue to use the variant, Tudur, to distinguish the medieval family from its post-medieval descendants.) Avidly loyal to King Henry V and a distinguished warrior, Owain gained a place at the king's court, probably as the keeper of

Queen Catherine's household. Taking the anglicised name, Owen Tudor, the Welshman secretly married the widowed queen in about 1431 and became step-father to the young Henry VI. Owen Tudor and Catherine of Valois had several children of their own, two of whom—Edmund and Jasper—played key roles in Harri Tudur's eventual accession to the throne.

In May 1461, shortly after the Yorkist victory at Towton, the soon-to-be King Edward IV assigned the task of subduing the county and lordship of Pembroke, and other portions of Wales and England, to Sir William Herbert of Raglan, whom he appointed as chief justiciar and chamberlain of South Wales. Shortly thereafter, Sir William also became Lord Herbert of Raglan, Chepstow and Gower. By July, Herbert and Sir Walter Devereux, Lord Ferrers, began assembling an army to invade South Wales and seize Jasper Tudur and Sir John Skydmore, who held Pembroke Castle on Tudur's behalf.

Finally, in September, the assault on Pembroke Castle began in earnest. While a fleet of ships sailed to Pembrokeshire to prevent the castle from receiving reinforcements or supplies, the Yorkist army made their way westward across southern Wales. They faced no resistance as they passed through Tenby to reach Pembroke, where a well-supplied Lancastrian garrison had anticipated their approach. However, rather than resist the swiftly advancing Yorkist army, Sir John Skydmore promptly surrendered in exchange for written guarantees of leniency. The documents were worthless, however, and King Edward IV quickly ordered Skydmore's attainder. Four year old Harri Tudur and his mother, Margaret Beaufort, were seized and imprisoned by the Yorkists, while their champion, Jasper Tudur, Earl of Pembroke, retreated to northern Wales, and, after a defeat near Caernarfon, fled to Ireland. As a reward for his service, Herbert received the lordships of Pembroke, Cilgerran and Walwyn's Castle (a sub-lordship) as well as four lordships in Carmarthenshire. The following year, Lord Herbert became Earl of Pembroke and also acquired the lordship of Haverford and its castles.

With the restoration of Henry VI in 1470 and the subsequent execution of William Herbert after the Battle of Edgecote, Jasper Tudur returned to Pembrokeshire to regain control of the earldom but was forced back into exile when Edward IV recovered his throne. Control of Pembrokeshire continued to shift between the Yorkists and Lancastrians, and in 1479 the Earl of Pembroke (William Herbert II) swapped the earldom and his other properties in Wales for those of the Earl of Huntingdon (Edward, the infant prince of Wales) in the West Country.

When the Duke of Gloucester became King Richard III in 1483, he granted Haverfordwest Castle and the lordship of Haverford, and also the lordships and castles of Narberth, Cilgerran and Llanstephan (in Carmarthenshire), to Edward Stafford, Duke of Buckingham, who had to relinquish his claim to the castles after participating in a failed rebellion against the king. Richard III's reign lasted only two years, and ended at Bosworth battlefield. Tradition has it that Richard was felled by the sword of Rhys ap Thomas, whom the new king, Henry VII, rewarded with a knighthood for his bravery. Rhys became the king's chamberlain of south Wales and also controlled most of Carmarthenshire and Cardiganshire.

In 1486, Henry VII bestowed the earldom of Pembroke once again on his uncle, Jasper, who retained the title and its privileges until his death in 1495. The king then transferred the lordships of Pembroke, Cilgerran and Haverford to his second son, Henry, Duke of York (the future Henry VIII), and kept the earldom of Pembroke inactive. In 1496, Henry VII appointed Sir Rhys ap Thomas as his justiciar of south Wales and, in 1505, he rewarded the Welshman's loyalty with a knighthood in the Order of the Garter.

Increasingly, as the kingdom settled into a period of internal peace, its castles acquired a more residential function. Attention and money were now lavished on domestic comfort and embellishment, while defensive features were neglected and allowed to decay. During the 1490s, Sir Rhys ap Thomas extended his influence by purchasing Carew Castle, which he transformed into a palatial showcase in honour of his king with the addition of heraldic crests dedicated to Henry VII, Prince Arthur, and the prince's new bride, Catherine of Aragon, a grandiose porchway into the great hall, and new living quarters.

When Henry VIII became king in 1509—Prince Arthur having died in 1502—he appointed Rhys ap Thomas as steward of Pembroke, and six years later confirmed Rhys as owner of Narberth

Castle. Sir Rhys continued to play a key role in the new king's government, serving on judicial and other commissions. Henry also tasked the Welshman with guarding Milford Haven and the sea route to Ireland from French invasion. At his death in 1525, Sir Rhys' grandson, Rhys ap Gruffydd, was poised to step into his grandfather's shoes (his father, Gruffydd, had died in 1521). However, the king considered the brash young man to be unreliable and appointed Walter Devereux, Lord Ferrers, as justiciar of south Wales, granting Devereux the position that Rhys believed was rightfully his. Rhys in turn became steward and receiver of Pembroke, and maintained an ongoing rivalry with Lord Ferrers that resulted, among other things, in accusations that the Welshman was scheming with the Scots to become king of Wales.

After a series of misadventures, including an unpopular attempt to expel Irish refugees from Tenby, imprisonment in Carmarthen Castle and in the Tower of London, Rhys was executed in 1531 for plotting to kill the king. In reality, Henry VIII felt threatened by the charismatic Welsh leader's loyalty to Rome during a time when he was seeking a way to rid himself of Catherine of Aragon and marry Anne Boleyn, for whom Rhys had an avowed dislike. After the execution, Rhys' wife, Catherine Howard, retained possession of the castle and sub-lordship of Carew until her death in 1554, when they reverted to the Crown.

In 1532, Henry VIII initiated a series of events that would forever change the nature of religious practice in Britain. In Wales the process included the creation of Anne Boleyn as marchioness of Pembroke. In 1534, Anne appointed William Barlow as Haverfordwest's prior, on the presumption that Barlow's political affinities and radical religious beliefs would facilitate the king's divorce from Catherine of Aragon and pending remarriage to Anne. In 1536, immediately after Barlow became Bishop of St Davids, he attempted to transfer the see from St Davids to Carmarthen, claiming Pembrokeshire was too removed from mainstream life. Barlow promptly abandoned the bishops' palaces at St Davids and Lamphey and his castellated residence at Cresswell in favour of the palace at Abergwili, Carmarthen.

Ever the zealous reformer, Bishop Barlow spearheaded the dissolution of the Welsh monasteries on behalf of his king, ordering the closure of the priory and friary at Haverfordwest in 1538. Within the next ten years, Barlow's brothers, Richard and Thomas, managed to procure both monastic complexes and also gained control of the Knights Hospitaller establishment at Slebech and the Tironensian community at Pill Priory, near Milford Haven. Bishop Barlow's plans to create a personal power base at Carmarthen ultimately failed, and, in 1548, he was transferred to the bishopric at Bath and Wells. When Mary Tudor rose to England's throne, she tried Barlow for heresy and executed him in 1555.

Besides the dissolution of the monasteries, Henry VIII also enacted the first Act of Union in 1536, which not only merged Wales with England, but also formally created the county (or shire) of Pembroke. The new administrative unit included the lands and castles of the earldom, the bishops of St Davids and the Hospitaller estates at Slebech. In 1543, the king declared Haverfordwest as a county unto itself (as Edward IV had done in 1479) and subdivided Pembrokeshire into seven smaller units, known as hundreds. The hundreds were Cemais, Cilgerran, Dewisland, Roose, Dungleddy, Narberth, and Castlemartin. Little England Beyond Wales then received administrative institutions roughly equivalent to those pertaining in English shires, but remained subject to control by the Council in the Marches of Wales based at Ludlow, Shropshire, rather than from London.

The gentry in Pembrokeshire, and elsewhere in the realm, were leaders in local society who had acquired substantial income and land holdings which gave them personal prestige and political power. They occupied key government offices, lived in impressive houses, and ruled the lower classes in the name of the monarchy. They also generally claimed noteworthy pedigrees which could be traced well back in time. The most influential and long-lasting gentry families in Pembrokeshire included the Wogans, Philipps, Stepneys, Owens, Bowens, Wyrriots and the Perrots. Of these families, the Perrots dominated not only the political scene in Pembrokeshire for several centuries but also held vast swathes of land in the county and in Haverfordwest itself.

The earliest known Perrot for whom we have documentary proof is Stephen Perrot who appears on a list of witnesses on a charter issued by de Valence in August 1290. It would seem, there-

31

fore, that the Perrots arrived in Wales after the defeat of Llywelyn ap Gruffudd, prince of Wales (k.1282) and that 'earlier' members of the family in Wales were a creation of Sir John Perrot who added three generations of Perrots to his family pedigree sometime in the mid-16th century. He also tried to prove a link between his supposed ancestor and the line of Hywel Dda! (Perrot was not alone in fictionalising his family origins, most of the gentry were at it. For example, Sir William Cecil, Lord Burghley, paid a Welsh herald to trace his family tree back to King Cadwaladr, a 6th-century Welsh king.) Even so, over time, the Perrots used a series of well-appointed marriages, land acquisitions and governmental offices to increase their political clout. By 1349, John Perrot's inquisition post mortem declared him to have countywide land holdings; also in the 14th century, Peter Perrot (d.1378) married Alice, the daughter of Sir Richard Harold of Haroldston, a manor just east of Haverfordwest. By the 1400s, Haroldston became the main seat of the Perrot family, whose branches were then scattered throughout Pembrokeshire, in Haverfordwest, Eastington, Scotsborough, Tenby and Narberth. During the 15th century, the Perrots and their cousins, the Wogans, dominated Pembrokeshire, occupying the offices of sheriff, steward and treasurer-chancellor for the county, other important positions and stately residences, such as Boulston House. In 1403, David Perrot of Tenby chose to support Owain Glyndwr, as noted earlier.

Of the Perrots, the controversial Elizabethan politician, Sir John Perrot, made arguably the greatest impact, not only in Pembrokeshire but also in royal circles. Rumoured but not proven to have been the illegitimate son of Henry VIII, Sir John Perrot was born in 1528, presumably at Haroldston, the ruins of which still survive. During his lengthy and remarkable career, Sir John, an avowed Protestant, served in the courts of Edward VI, Mary Tudor and Elizabeth I. Mary granted Perrot extensive estates in Pembrokeshire, including Carew Castle, plus other properties elsewhere in Wales and in England as well. Allegations that he had harboured heretics landed Sir John in prison but he was released upon Queen Mary's request.

During the reign of Queen Elizabeth, Sir John Perrot served as Vice-Admiral of South Wales, Keeper of Haverfordwest gaol,

Member of Parliament, Mayor of Haverfordwest, Lord President of Munster, Member of the Council in the Marches, Lord Deputy of Ireland, Deputy Lord Lieutenant of Pembrokeshire, and Privy Councillor. Perrot's sometimes boisterous and always ambitious nature inevitably caused problems for him both in Ireland, where new English settlers began to resist his control over their lands, and in Wales and England, where questions were raised about his loyalties during England's conflict with Spain. In 1591, Perrot found himself imprisoned in the Tower of London, indicted for fomenting rebellion, conspiring with King Philip II of Spain and slandering Elizabeth I. Once one of the queen's favourite courtiers, Sir John Perrot apparently died from natural causes while awaiting execution in the Tower.

Sir John Perrot's claim to fame stems both from his tumultuous career, which frequently ignited the fury of his local gentry class rivals, and also from his lasting legacy to Haverfordwest: the bequest of 'certain messuages, lands, tenements, burgages and hereditaments within and without the town' in 1580 to establish the charity now known as the Sir John Perrot Trust. The list of properties that Perrot owned at that time is astounding. It included farmland in Camrose and Wolfsdale, two villages north of Haverfordwest, numerous houses, gardens, stables, and storehouses spread throughout Haverfordwest itself. Today, the recently restored almshouses lining Perrot's Terrace in Haverfordwest remain the property of the Trust.

Perrot also managed to transform his castles at Carew and Laugharne, in Carmarthenshire, into Elizabethan mansions. His most impressive contribution at Carew is the three-storeyed northern façade, which overlooks the Carew River. Now little more than a glorious shell, the structure featured five rooms, including a long gallery with two rows of huge mullioned window frames and two large oriel windows. With the addition of the northern range, builders completed the castle's transformation from military stronghold to lavish Elizabethan residence. Sadly, he died in the Tower before he could occupy the castle.

The Perrots influenced Pembrokeshire's political scene well into the late 17th century. Sir Thomas Perrot, John's eldest son, served as mayor in 1586, and another son, Sir James Perrot, played a key role in local efforts to prevent coastal piracy, as had his father before him. Increasingly, landholders from other prominent gentry families gained control in Pembrokeshire, including Robert Devereux, the second Earl of Essex, who—for a time—became another of Elizabeth I's favourites. The last Perrot to hold any political sway in the county was Sir Herbert, who inherited Haroldston but was not directly related to the Pembrokeshire branch of the family. In 1677, Sir Herbert began a term as Member for Parliament for Haverfordwest.

IV Decline and Restoration

By the end of the 16th century, the construction of new castles had ceased in Pembrokeshire. Extant castles had received makeovers, and many now accommodated their owners in grand style and a greater degree of comfort than previously experienced. Nonetheless, the stone fortresses remained in solid enough condition that, when the Civil War erupted in the 1640s, they were garrisoned and saw action. Pembroke Castle became a thorn in the side of both Royalist and Parliamentarian forces, and, in 1648, Oliver Cromwell himself besieged the castle.

While most of Wales supported King Charles I, the people of Pembrokeshire were divided between the Royalist and Parliamentary causes. In southern Pembrokeshire, several gentry families became vigorous champions for Parliament. Basing themselves at Pembroke, the well-organised group essentially ignored directives issued by the Royalists and established their own Parliamentary administration. In response to a demand from Parliament in August 1642, they appointed 16 local baronets and esquires as county commissioners. The commissioners had the power to muster a militia, stockpile arms and secure all strongpoints against the Royalists. Most of Pembrokeshire, meanwhile, claimed they stood for the king, but few intervened on his behalf. Indeed, many of the county's strongholds shifted allegiances several times, and participated in little or no real fighting.

By the end of 1642, Charles I had established a series of pro-Royalist administrations throughout Wales, except for southern Pembrokeshire, and appointed Richard Vaughan, Earl of Carbery, of Golden Grove, Carmarthenshire, as commander in West Wales. The king's pro-Parliamentary opponents in Pembrokeshire had garrisoned and readied Pembroke, Tenby and Haverfordwest to fight the Royalist army, but it took almost another year for the conflict to get underway. In August and September 1643, Haverfordwest and Tenby submitted with little resistance. As Pembroke remained defiant, the town's seizure became Carbery's main objective. Captain William Smith's Parliamentary forces captured two Royalist ships anchored in Milford Haven, and shortly thereafter Admiral Richard Swanley and his fleet of ships secured the waterway for Parliament. By summer's end, Carbery had planted Royalist garrisons at Haverfordwest, Tenby, Carew, Manorbier, Roch, and several prominent residences, but Parliamentarians commanded by Colonel Rowland Laugharne, maintained their grip on Pembroke Castle.

To smash the Parliamentary hold on Pembroke and block provisioning by sea, Carbery's men began building an artillery fort at Pill, near the town of Milford. In early 1644, Laugharne responded with assaults on the garrisons at Stackpole and Trefloyne. Aided by Admiral Swanley's ships, which patrolled the Irish Sea, Laugharne then stormed Pill. The Royalists fled Pembrokeshire altogether, and Tenby and Haverfordwest became Parliamentary strongholds. After failing to provide support for Trefloyne, Carbery was relieved of his command in April and replaced by Charles Gerard.

In May 1644, Gerard led 2,000 Royalist soldiers into southwestern Wales. After almost 12 weeks, he had recaptured most of the region, including Roch and Haverfordwest, installed several garrisons around the county, and instigated a 'scorched earth' policy in an effort to force the Parliamentarians out of Pembroke and Tenby. Ironically, before he could effect a victory, Gerard and his men had to return to England to fight for their king. In their absence, Parliamentarian troops retook all of Pembrokeshire and lands as far east as Carmarthenshire, taking Laugharne Castle without a struggle.

In early 1645, Gerard again marched into Pembrokeshire, killing or capturing over 500 pro-Parliamentarians while seizing Haverfordwest, Picton, Carew, and smaller strongholds. Tenby and Pembroke remained beyond his reach. After regrouping and organising a force estimated to include 500 foot soldiers, 200 horse and dragoons, and two small guns from the arsenals at Pembroke and Tenby, Rowland Laugharne led his Parliamentarian troops to

Canaston Wood, a few miles east of Haverfordwest, where they captured several Royalist lookouts. Here they were also joined by some 250 additional men, who had sailed up the River Cleddau and disembarked nearby, and the combined Parliamentarian force then headed towards Llawhaden. On 1 August 1645 they encountered the Royalist army of 1,500 foot and horse and four cannons at nearby Colby Moor. After an hour of fighting, the underdog Parliamentarians defeated the Royalists, killing 150 and taking 700 prisoners. Major-Generals Stradling and Egerton, who had remained behind at Haverfordwest Castle, fled to Carmarthen, leaving their Royalist garrison to fend for themselves. Colonel Laugharne then marched to Haverfordwest with his men and, after a short siege, seized Haverfordwest Castle, burnt its gatehouse, and captured the defenders. During the affray, the Parliamentarians reportedly only lost two men, and 60 others were wounded. Shortly afterwards they also retook Carew and Manorbier. Finally, in September, Picton Castle's Royalist garrison surrendered after a 20-day siege, which marked the current end of fighting in Pembrokeshire. Fighting in the rest of Wales ceased in 1646.

Even though the Civil War had ended for all intents and purposes, the unstable political situation sparked further rebellion in 1648. In south-western Wales, Pembroke and its castle became the focal point of the rekindled rebellion. Dismayed with the appointments of several pro-Royalists to the local government, John Poyer, mayor of Pembroke, refused to step down when Colonel Fleming, Parliamentary commander, arrived to take charge of the castle. Rowland Laugharne and Colonel Rice Powell came to Poyer's aid, and all three now sided with their King against Parliament. They forced Fleming and his army out of Pembrokeshire, followed that with a rout of Parliamentary troops led by Colonel Reade, and then thwarted an assault by Colonel Horton and his men. The newly avowed Royalists also seized Tenby and Carmarthen and then made their way eastward towards Cardiff. At St Fagans, Horton's army captured 3,000 rebels, but the Royalist leaders, Powell, Poyer and Laugharne, managed to flee to safety in Pembrokeshire.

Late in May, Lieutenant-General Oliver Cromwell arrived in Pembrokeshire with 6,000 men. In early June, as Cromwell began his offensive against Pembroke, Tenby and its commander, Rice

Powell, fell to the Parliamentarians. The siege of Pembroke Castle continued for six weeks. The attackers attempted to starve out the garrison, but delays in the arrival of Cromwell's siege train almost ended in disaster for the besiegers, who were themselves on the verge of starvation. On 4 June, the Parliamentarians stormed the castle's walls but lost 23 men in the fray. Then, a sudden sortie from inside the castle killed or injured 29 more of the attackers, but also led to the wounding of Colonel Laugharne. Cromwell's troops then had brief success when they breached the town walls, pushed the Royalist troops back into the castle and killed 100 defenders. In the meantime, however, Laugharne and his men, who had held fast at the eastern gateway into Pembroke, took advantage of the situation to promptly stage a rear attack against the Parliamentarians. They rushed up what is now Main Street towards the castle, where they killed about 30 of the besiegers and forced the rest to retreat.

The siege of Pembroke Castle then reached a stalemate until Cromwell's heavy artillery arrived in late June. By then, lighter guns had battered the castle, and morale waned. After four days, Laugharne and Poyer requested surrender terms from Cromwell. On 10 July, the Royalists yielded. Some opted to leave the country; others quietly returned to their homes. Laugharne, Poyer and Powell were hauled to London and condemned to death. Poyer's name was chosen by a drawing of lots, and, in April 1649, he was executed by firing squad. Laugharne and Powell were released 12 days later.

During this second phase of the Civil War, the garrisons at two of Pembrokeshire's castles erected defensive siege works in an effort to keep the Parliamentarians at bay. Outside the main gate to Manorbier Castle they constructed a stone-revetted redan, which protected the northeastern side of the castle. At Carew they planted a V-shaped bank, known as a ravelin, before Sir Rhys ap Thomas' 16th-century gatehouse. Other Civil War features at Carew include small musket holes piercing the high wall near the entrance into the inner ward. Blocked windows in the great hall provided a barrier of sorts behind which the defenders could fire their muskets with relative safety. Musketballs were also unearthed during recent excavations.

Between 1648 and 1649, Oliver Cromwell as Lord Protector ordered the slighting of scores of castles. His army pulled down the entire southern range and curtain wall at Carew Castle. At

Pembroke, they set off charges of gunpowder along the outer curtain wall. Except for the Barbican Tower, which survives just east of the great gatehouse, the façades of every tower suffered extensive damage. Battlements were also blown apart. At Haverfordwest, Cromwell ordered the townspeople to slight their castle. Claiming they lacked financial resources, adequate tools and manpower to complete the effort, they only conducted a cursory assault on the castle. Manorbier Castle survived the Civil War almost intact; only the battlements were damaged during slighting. After the Civil War, the owners of Carew and Narberth castles abandoned their strongholds in favour of grander dwellings. Picton, on the other hand, continued its role as a residence for the landed gentry, and today remains in fine condition. Haverfordwest Castle became a substantial prison, and in 1797 held French prisoners captured during the 'Last Invasion of Wales', which took place at Carreg Wasted, near Fishguard. Twenty years later, the castle imprisoned debtors and housed two working treadmills, one fitted for men and the other for women. Some fortified residences, like Eastington, were incorporated into later structures which protected their medieval fabric, while others, like Haroldston, await essential consolidation.

By the 19th century, Pembrokeshire's decaying fortresses were in dire need of consolidation and protection. Fortunately, attitudes towards preservation changed, and ruins began to be viewed as valuable for the role they played in the nation's history. Antiquarian J.R. Cobb was especially captivated by castles in Wales, and played a key role in their restoration during the 1880s. Living for a time at Manorbier Castle, Cobb restored the floors inside the towers and the gatehouse, added new windows, consolidated the masonry, and also built a private residence within the grounds. At Pembroke, he rebuilt the barbican and main gatehouse and excavated the horseshoe gate. He also carried out restoration work at Carew and Caldicot castles.

In the early 20th century, Sir Ivor Philipps completed Cobb's restoration of Pembroke Castle. Sir Ivor's descendant, Sheila Philipps (Lady Dunsany), took a special interest in Manorbier Castle, the preservation of which she spearheaded until her death in 1999. In the 1930s, Ernest Pegge rebuilt Benton Castle, retaining much of its original masonry. The structure has since remained a private home. The crumbling Roch Castle was also renovated during the 20th century and is now open to the public as self-catering accommodation.

Besides a plethora of medieval castles, Pembrokeshire has its share of shams, castle-like residences built in modern times and intended for use as private homes rather than for any military purpose. Upton Castle, for example, is one, built in the 19th century on the site of an earlier medieval structure, of which only a small portion has survived. Visitors will find the lush gardens and restored medieval chapel of more interest. At Amroth, people often mistake the modern sham 'castle'—which is in the centre of a caravan park—as the original, but the stone sham was actually built in the early 19th century. Amroth's medieval castle, a motte, still overlooks Carmarthen Bay at the edge of a grassy field on the hills above the sham.

The current conditions of Pembrokeshire's castles vary from completely vanished, as at Begelly and Castlemorris, to eroded but solid, as at Wiston, to restored but still greatly ruined, as at Haverfordwest, to heavily restored, as at Pembroke. Regardless of the condition, each played a role in the history of the region, and as such is priceless. Some are undergoing routine maintenance, thanks to the efforts of Trusts, Cadw and private citizens. Others are undergoing archaeological investigation, which will only enhance their inherent value and our understanding of the past. Excavations have been ongoing for decades at Carew, and Narberth recently received a major facelift. Both projects produced unexpected findings. Recent excavations at Lydstep have also provided new insight into the site. Re-examination of the building phases at Pembroke Castle has led to new theories about who erected the original castle, whether or not an earthwork castle actually stood at the site, and whether the Marshals or de Valences were responsible for the extensive masonry upgrade. Clearance and consolidation work completed at Angle, Wiston and St Davids Bishops' Palace now allow increased public access and have engendered greater insight into the medieval significance of the sites. However, uncertainty persists about the typology of many of the earthwork castles (are they mottes, ringworks, hillforts—or even barrows), which can only be confirmed with excavation. While arguably not as visually stimulating as their masonry counterparts, motte and ringwork castles require as great an investment of archaeological attention as the stone fortresses.

Amroth

Motte
Location: Near the church above the village (SN 163 077)
Access: Can be seen from a private track

Take the road away from the shore by the inn in Amroth and drive
carefully up the narrow lane until you reach the church of St. Elidir
above the village and park at the church car park. Walk back up the
short rise towards Amroth and turn left on to the private track opposite the farm buildings near the crest of the rise. After a few hundred
yards the motte is visible on the right. Please note that you should
ask permission from the farmer to use this track.

Certainly, the crumbling battlemented eyesore that hubs a
sprawling caravan park in the centre of Amroth village looks like a
castle. Indeed, it is called Amroth Castle, and is acknowledged by
all too many writers as the site of the medieval castle that once
existed here—but it was built in about 1800 by Captain James
Ackland.

Situated on farmland overlooking Carmarthen Bay, the
medieval motte castle at Amroth is presently very overgrown with
underbrush, bracken and grasses. What appear to be dressed and
rough stone are scattered on and around the circular motte, and

masonry foundations of what may have been a tower can be seen on the east and northern sides of the mound. Erosion and burrowing animals have degraded the motte, and scrap metal and trash litter much of the site.

Variously known as Amroath, Ambroth, and Amboth, there is some evidence that the castle may have been constructed by the de Say family or by Cadwgan ap Bleddyn, prince of Powys, who married the de Say heiress (possibly Frances de Say). Cadwgan died *c*.1111. Some historians claim that this castle was the site of a banquet held by Cadwgan in honour of local leaders, including Gerald de Windsor, lord of Carew Castle and constable of Pembroke Castle. After the feast, the Welshman's son, Owain ap Cadwgan, rushed to Cilgerran Castle (see separate entry) and allegedly kidnapped the irresistible Nest, the daughter of Rhys ap Tewdwr who was also Windsor's Welsh-born wife, while Gerald fled to safety down a latrine chute.

In the 14th century ownership of Amroth Castle passed to the Elliot family, who apparently built a new stone castle, then called Earwere, Earweare or Erwer, closer to the bay. It may be this castle that the modern, better publicised pile replaced.

Angle

Tower House
Location: In Angle (SM 866 030)
Access: Exterior freely visible, interior open during the summer
or by special arrangement through Castle Farm

The Tower House is located near the centre of the village, to the left of the road that heads to Angle Bay.

Also called Nangle, Angle is nestled at the north-western tip of the Castlemartin Peninsula. The four-storey fortified tower house commands attention at the northern edge of the small village and you can park adjacent to the school and opposite the post office. To reach the tower house follow the foot worn path that cuts across the soggy grass, part of the rectangular area that once would have been enclosed by a stone wall, most of which has long since disappeared. The marshy spot alongside the stream probably once carried the tower's water supply and would have filled the stone-lined moat at high tide. Traces of a smaller corner tower still survive, but are difficult to spot when brush grows tall.

While some have claimed that the placename derives from the Norse *ongull*, 'fiord' or 'a hook', in the early 19th century, Richard

Fenton concurred with ancient deeds that described the spot as being *in angulo*, meaning in a nook or corner of land. However, the name may also refer to early landowners in the area. Once part of the Hundred of Castlemartin and the Earldom of Pembroke, the de Nangles (or de Angulos) were lords of the manor that includes modern-day Angle. In 1278, Philip de Angulo granted the manorial lands to Robert de Shirburn (Sherbourne/Sherborne), who had married Isobel de Angulo and acquired the property by right of marriage.

Angle's prime location at the mouth of Milford Haven has made it popular with seafarers and fishermen, but also vulnerable to invasion. Most likely, Angle Castle was built in the late 14th century, when the Shirburns recognised the need to improve the defensive capabilities of their home due to ongoing tensions with the French resulting from the Hundred Years War. In 1405 during the Glyndwr rebellion, French supporters landed near Angle, *en route* to a rendezvous with the legendary freedom fighter.

Harkening more to Irish or Scottish origins, Angle Castle is the only structure of its kind left in Wales. Rising about 10.5 metres high and constructed with walls 1 metre thick, Angle's machicolated tower house provided single living chambers, measuring three metres square, on each of the upper three floors. The ground level had a vaulted ceiling and was probably used for storage. The main entrance was at first floor level, and apparently a movable drawbridge allowed visitors to gain access. Surface evidence indicates that a porch or staircase and forebuilding may have been added. Once inside, travel from floor to floor was accomplished by using the corner spiral staircase—the rounded turret holding the stairs is noticeable from the outside at the tower's north-eastern corner. Each chamber had its own fireplace, small unglazed windows and arrow loops, but only the first floor was equipped with a garderobe. Corbels still rim the roof line.

For decades, the tower house was also known as the Old Rectory, and early Ordnance Survey maps highlight this name rather than its more appropriate designation, 'tower'. At least one OS map used 'castle' to label the tower house, which is more suitable than 'rectory'. Although no garrison guarded the structure, the site was a stronghold in which the Shirburns could feel at least a moderate sense of safety if an enemy approached. Tower houses of this style were commonly built in Scotland and Ireland to defend their owners from raids or swift attacks from locals, including rival clans. They abound along the borders between Scotland and England, and exist throughout Ireland.

The possibility is strong that the Irish influenced the design of Angle's tower house, and perhaps also the medieval building behind the post office, which bears a close resemblance to an Irish hall-house. This coastal nook was a convenient landing point for many more people than just the French, and it seems reasonable that the town was a base for travel to and from Ireland. If the Shirburns had travelled to Ireland, they would have had ample opportunity to see tower houses and bring the design concept back with them to use for their own home.

Situated beyond the tower house and partly hidden from view, Angle's recently restored dovecote evokes notions of the harshness of medieval life, even for people of status. Providing row upon row of pigeon holes for the birds to live in, the Shirburns harvested pigeons as a convenient source of fresh meat for their winter meals. Similar dovecotes are found elsewhere in Pembrokeshire, for example, at Manorbier, Monkton and Rosemarket.

The second substantial medieval structure in Angle has variously been called a 'nunnery', 'castle' and 'semi-fortified domestic building'. However, as of yet, no one has identified the exact nature of this blocky edifice. Today, access to this square stone structure behind the post office is restricted, being on private property and watched over by the resident sheepdog. Originally, the building consisted of two storeys, separated by a heavy timber floor. The first floor chamber had windows, a fireplace and a cupboard with a stone shelf, while the ground floor storeroom was lit with narrow windows, which would have prohibited enemy access.

The Royal Commission on Ancient and Historical Monuments in Wales (RCAHMW) has described the structure as a 'Ruined Almshouse'. The only documentation to support this conclusion is a comment in diocesan records from 1715, which stated: 'There is a ... ruined almshouse at Angle and £30 left by the will of Griffith

The blocky possible first-floor hall behind the post office

Dawes, Esq. of Barneston [Bangeston] near 40 years since, but no part thereof is yet paid by his administrators towards the repair thereof'. From the building's present appearance, it looks as if the will administrators never did make reparations.

Legends claim that the medieval manor at Angle was divvied up between the three female heiresses of one of the Shirburns, each of whom built an impressive home. One daughter gained the lordship of the manor and erected the tower house and its fortified enclosure on the northern side of the village. The second daughter built another fortified home, possibly the squat ruin behind the village post office. The third home no longer exists, but may have stood on the site just outside the village now occupied by the Hall.

Whatever the truth of the legend, the manor of Angle did eventually pass out of the hands of the Shirburns. For a time, Sir John Perrot had possession of the place. At Perrot's death in 1592, ownership passed to Walter Rees, then to John Kynner, Lord Cawdor, who controlled most of the lands on the Castlemartin Peninsula, and then to other owners. For a time, the site also incorporated a masonry inn. In 1805, John Mirehouse purchased the estates. Now privately owned, Angle's tower house has recently been restored with the assistance of Cadw.

Begelly

Now vanished probable motte
Location: (SN 117 072)

There is some written evidence that Begelly once had an earthwork castle at the centre of the medieval manor of Begelly, and that the last remnants of the site were removed in 1955. Clearly, nothing remains in the village today to prove a castle of any kind once stood at the site, which more than likely would have been located not too far from the church, which does survive.

Benton

Enclosure Castle
Location: Above the River Cleddau, 6 miles east of
Milford Haven (SN 005 069)
Access: Private, but can be seen from public footpath

A footpath passes the castle site and provides a chance to view the white-painted edifice. In the village of Houghton take Rhoose Ferry Road off to the east (from near a public telephone kiosk). Follow this along till you reach a drive and public footpath combined off to the left for Benton Farm. Park near here (but not so as to obstruct lorries using the drive), and walk up the drive/footpath. Just past the first set of farm buildings on the right, walk along the footpath that passes in front of the farmhouse and out into the field beyond. Follow the track alongside the field boundary on your right and onto the track through the woodland at the far side of the field. This soon leads out into a field which you then cross on much the same line to join another track on the far side. Turn right on this and at the end of the field, as the path starts to turn to the right, you can see the white painted castle in the grounds of a private house on the left.

Perched on an outcrop of volcanic rock, compact Benton Castle overlooks the River Cleddau, near its junction with the Rivers Carew and Cresswell. Little is known for certain of its medieval origins, however, most likely the first stone castle at the site existed in the late 13th century, when it would have been subordinate to the barony at Walwyn's Castle (see separate entry). Debate exists over the builders of the castle, who may have been either the de la Roches (de la Rupes), who had a similar stronghold at Roch (see separate entry). By the end of the century, the castle was the property of Bishop Thomas Bek, whose main residence was the Bishops Palace at St Davids (see separate entry). During the 16th century Benton Castle was the property of Sir John Perrot, said to have been the half-brother of Queen Elizabeth I.

The present castellated structure probably incorporates the remains of the original stone castle and may approximate the medieval layout. Ernest Pegge rebuilt the decaying castle in the 1930s and it has remained a private home since then.

The attractive building consisted of two round towers flanking a simple arched gateway which opened to an irregularly shaped inner ward enclosed by a battlemented curtain wall. There is some speculation, based on the plan of the site, that the original castle was a ringwork. The taller of the two towers rises three storeys, measures 7.5 metres in diameter and is crowned with octagonal battlements which apparently retrace the medieval design but are a modern restoration. Access between the floors appears to have been via movable ladders. The structure itself lacked fireplaces but was equipped with a latrine tower projecting from its west-facing side. A doorway at the second level offered access to the wall-walk, which crossed over the weakly defended gate passage (no portcullis) to link with the smaller tower, which had a diameter of about five metres. Walls measure about three metres in thickness. At one time the curtain wall enclosed the courtyard into which the gateway opened.

Caldey Priory

Fortified Tower
Location: On Caldey Island (SN 141 963)
Access: Privately owned, open daily from Easter
until the end of October

The tower is located alongside a footpath that leads southwards across the island from the current monastery.

Caldey Island, off the southern coast of Pembrokeshire near Tenby, has a long association with monasticism. Today, the island is owned and managed by Cistercian monks who live there and worship in the rebuilt abbey church that dominates the scenic island. In the 5th century during the so-called Age of the Saints, Celtic Christians probably established a clas, or small religious community, on the island, which was then known as Ynys Pyr (Pyro's Island). Inscribed stones dating from that time provide solid evidence of their presence on Caldey. While 9th-century carved stones have also been found at Caldey, it is difficult to determine whether the island was occupied continuously after the 5th century. However, during the early 12th century, Ynys Pyr appears in the historical record. In 1113, Henry I granted possession to Robert FitzMartin, Lord of Cemmaes (see entry on Nevern Castle). Robert in turn gave Caldey to his mother, Geva, who founded a priory shortly thereafter. Caldey Priory was established as a cell of the Benedictine monastery at St Dogmael's, near Cardigan, which her son had established in 1115. The extensive remains of that site are accessible to the public.

Construction on Caldey Priory began in the 13th century, and featured a central cloister-garth surrounded by the standard monastic buildings: the church, dedicated to St Illtyd, stood to the south; the monks' dormitory and calefactory were built below and to the east of the church; guest accommodation stood to the west, on the opposite side of the main gatehouse from the church; and the refectory (no longer standing) once existed to the north.

Standing at the north-eastern corner of the site between the rectory and the dormitory was, arguably, Caldey Priory's most noteworthy feature, the Prior's Tower. The battlemented square tower not only housed the prior but also offered him some protection from raiding pirates. Completed in the 14th century, the Prior's Tower remains in excellent condition. Internally, the two-storey tower measures 5.5 metres by 4.5 metres, and has walls over one metre in thickness. Accessed via an external timber stairway, the prior's simple first floor chamber was fitted with a fireplace and small latrine turret; the vaulted basement may have served as the prior's kitchen, and had a separate entrance at the south-western corner.

Caldey remained an active priory until Henry VIII's dissolution of the monasteries, which began in 1536. The king granted the island and other church properties (including St Dogmael's) to John Bradshawe of Presteigne. In 1612, the Bradshawes sold Caldey Island to Walter Philpin, mayor of Tenby, whose descendants in turn sold the site to the Williams family of Llanrhidian and Loughor in 1653. Ownership of the island and its crumbing religious buildings changed hands several times during the 18th and 19th centuries, and in 1906, it again became the property of the Benedictines. However, it was not until after the Second World War that the monastery saw a rebirth, when Cistercian monks took over Caldey Island and transformed it back into a successful working religious community, but on a new site towards the northern shore.

Boats run from Tenby Harbour to the island every 20 minutes.

Camrose

Motte and Bailey
Location: In the village of Camrose (SM 927 198)
Access: Can be seen from the road

Camouflaged by trees and the steep sides of a lengthy lane that winds northwards from the A487 to the compact but expanding hamlet of Camrose, the massive motte belies its grander origins. Now severed by the modern C-road which followed the line of the castle ditch, the hulking motte and sprawling bailey were probably built alongside Camrose Brook in the very late 11th century. However, nothing of the site's history is documented prior to 1188, when Gerald of Wales (Giraldus Cambrensis) passed through the area with Archbishop Baldwin seeking converts for the Third Crusade.

Rising almost 8 metres high, the motte once supported stone walls, the presence of which may indicate that the summit was crowned by a shell keep. In the 18th century, the mound became the focal point of an elaborate garden constructed to showcase the neighbouring manor house, which has been occupied by the Bowens, Webb-Bowens and Penns, lords of the manor and vicars at the parish church of St. Ishmael, located uphill from the castle. During the transformation, the motte acquired the spiral terracing that still traces its sides.

The three-storey Georgian residence that replaced the original manor house is now the home of the Vaughans, local squires. Across the brook and nestled in the sweeping curve across from the driveway leading to Camrose House, a corn mill served the earls of Pembroke as early as 1324, and was still in working order in the early 20th century. It has since been restored and is used as a private residence.

Carew (Caeriw)

Enclosure Castle
Location: In the village of Carew, north-east of Pembroke
(SN 163 077)
Access: Managed by the Pembrokeshire Coast National Park
Authority, with whom check for opening times

The hulking grey ruins of Carew Castle command a promontory jutting out into the River Carew, which flows to the north and the west and once allowed seagoing vessels to pass with ease according to the day's tidal fluctuations. Well situated for communication and to receive supplies, the river formed a natural moat around Carew Castle. Today, the castle sits serenely alongside the village, which features several interesting historical monuments of its own including the remains of a 'Flemish' chimney in one front yard and the great wheel-headed cross, which now overlooks the A4075 immediately to the east of the castle grounds.

Carew Castle and its surrounding lands have been the focus of ongoing archaeological excavation for almost 20 years. Not only have they revealed significant medieval remains at Carew, but archaeologists have also unearthed a series of rock-cut ditches and ramparts on the eastern side of the castle. The presence of the ditches indicates that the spot may have supported a settlement of some kind as early as the Iron Age. Artefacts uncovered during the excavations included Roman era pottery and brooches and other finds dating to the early Middle Ages.

The Carew Cross dates to the 11th century, when the princes of Deheubarth ruled the area. The incised stone actually bears an inscription dedicated to Maredudd ab Edwin, who ruled the region with his brother Hywel, and was killed in 1035. As recent archaeological findings suggest, the presence of this great stone cross may have more relevance to the history of the neighbouring castle than was once recognised. Although the Carew Cross is not in its original position, its survival may indicate that the site was continuously occupied from the Iron Age until the late 11th century, when the Normans moved into the area.

Located on the eastern, inland side of the masonry castle in an area occupied later by the outer ward of the castle, is a much older series of five or six deep ditches, arranged in parallel lines which were cut into the bedrock and protected by earth and stone ramparts. Traces of a timber gatehouse have also been unearthed. The ditches would have provided effective defence for an Iron Age promontory fort at the site, and may indicate the first of many occupation periods at Carew.

When Gerald de Windsor, constable of Pembroke Castle (see separate entry), married Nest, the daughter of Rhys ap Tewdwr, Prince of Deheubarth, he acquired Carew and the adjoining lands as part of his new wife's dowry. (Besides Carew, Gerald also had a castle at Cilgerran — see separate entry). Shortly thereafter, Gerald probably replaced whatever kind of residence Nest's family may have occupied at Carew with his own rudimentary castle in the early 12th century. He probably levelled the Iron Age ramparts and infilled the ditches, except for a section that still lines the eastern side of the castle immediately north of the outer gatehouse. But the remains of Gerald's castle no longer exist. Some historians speculate that the first Norman castle at Carew was a motte castle, while others believe it would have been a ringwork, but there is no firm evidence for either type of structure at the site. The later masonry

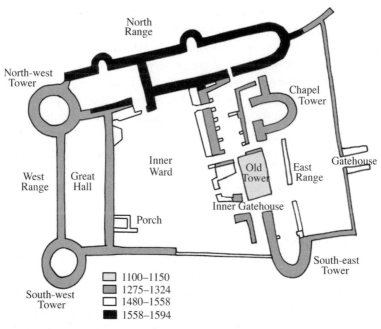

North
Range

North-west
Tower

Chapel
Tower

Inner
Ward

West
Range

Great
Hall

Old
Tower

East
Range

Gatehouse

Inner Gatehouse

Porch

South-east
Tower

□ 1100–1150
■ 1275–1324
□ 1480–1558
■ 1558–1594

South-west
Tower

Plan of Carew Castle

castle was essentially rectilinear in design, fronted with a large outer bailey on the eastern side, and protected with four corner towers. Over time, modifications were made to the plan, new towers added along the eastern and southern walls and a new façade added on the northern side. Ultimately, Carew Castle combined military and trendy decorative features into a strong yet very attractive fortified residence that was accessed via at least three separate gateways.

The first actual mention of a castle here dates to 1212, when the *domus of Carrio* appears in the historical record, having been seized by King John, who was passing through Pembrokeshire *en route to* Ireland. By this time, the property had passed to William FitzGerald, Gerald and Nest's son, who had adopted the surname *Carrio* or 'Carew', which was thenceforth passed to his descendants. In Welsh, the name translates to *Caeriw*, and may derive from *caer rhiw* or 'fort on a small hill'. The pronunciation of the word and its location overlooking the River Carew lend considerable credibility to this association. Alternatively, the surname may derive from *caerau*, the plural form of *caer* or 'fort'.

Sir Nicholas de Carew, who fought with Edward I in both North Wales and Scotland, inherited the castle in the late 13th century. He added his own legacy by constructing the impressive western range of buildings with its two enormous angle towers and great hall. Much of what survives dates to this building programme. Sir Nicholas was buried at Carew Cheriton Church, located near the junction of the A4075 and A477 just south of the castle.

The oldest surviving masonry structure at Carew Castle is the so-called Old Tower, which dates to the 12th century. This tower was incorporated into later construction when the inner gatehouse and eastern range of buildings were added in the latter part of the 13th century, probably by Sir Nicholas de Carew. When viewed from the exterior, the structure is still identifiable by its distinctive masonry. Possibly built by Gerald de Windsor, or more likely by his son, William, to serve as the first gatehouse into the castle, the structure originally rose three storeys and had a latrine chute on the first floor. In the latter part of the 12th century, the entrance in the old tower was blocked, and a new, albeit very simple, gateway was opened in the walling immediately to the south. Fitted with arrowslits, murder holes, a portcullis and heavy timber doors, the new gateway was actually well equipped for a defensive role.

The Old Tower and east range

On the south side of the newer gateway (which now serves as the main entrance into the interior of the castle), the D-shaped south-eastern tower projects farther outward into the outer bailey than the gateway. Probably added during a major building programme conducted by Sir Nicholas de Carew and his son, John, in the late 13th century, the flat, eastern side of this tower contained latrines, among other items. The expanse of curtain wall adjoining this tower on the western side was almost completely destroyed during the English Civil War in the 17th century. It once featured a square turret and kitchen tower, both located about midway along the wall, but only traces of the two buildings survive.

On the northern side of the old tower, Sir Nicholas constructed the eastern range of buildings, which included the lesser hall and the massive chapel tower. Much of this building has been revamped for use during special events at the castle. The eastern hall occupied the first floor above a vaulted undercroft, and would have been used by de Carew for small, private functions. The side facing into the inner ward was modified in the 16th century, when new mullioned windows were added. Linked to the lesser hall by a narrow passageway, the chapel tower held the steward's room, which had its own garderobe, and the kitchen, adorned with ribbed vaulting on ground level.

Polygonal in plan, the battlemented chapel tower stood three storeys high and jutted out into the outer ward. The chapel itself occupied the first floor. It features cross-ribbed vaulting as well as an aumbry for storing vessels used during mass and a piscina. A tiny private room located just off this main room would have been used by the priest for his own purposes, including preparing for mass. This room still contains its fireplace and window with seat. A latrine beyond would have accommodated the priest. Another private chamber, probably the lord's solar, occupies the uppermost storey. Its decorative fireplace displays the arms of King Henry VII, which would have been added when Rhys ap Thomas owned the castle in the 16th century.

On the opposite side of the inner ward stands the impressive western block, which contained the great hall and showcased the owners' wealth and status. Measuring 25 metres by 8 metres, and having walls some three metres thick, the first floor hall was certainly an impressive building. Standing above a vaulted undercroft probably used for storage, the great hall occupied the entire first floor of the building, had an open timber roof, and featured two huge fireplaces, a minstrels' gallery on the south, and elaborately carved windows.

To either side of the great hall stand the foreboding remains of two massive spur towers, which face the river and would have offered powerful resistance to any waterborne assault. Also built by Sir

The south-western tower

Nicholas de Carew, the well-preserved battlemented towers stand three storeys high, stretch 10.5 metres in diameter, and are supported on square bases with pyramidal spurs. Each tower contains a vaulted basement and two upper storeys, which provided additional accommodation, contained fireplaces, garderobes and large windows, and were reached from the great hall via a set of stairs. These towers are best viewed from across the river.

During the mid-15th century, William Carew, brother of Sir Thomas Carew, then owner of the castle, had married the heiress of Sir Hugh Courtney of Haccombe, in the West Country. Consequently, the Carews extended their holdings into Devon and Somerset, and moved into Crowcombe Court, where their descendants, the Trollope-Bellews, still reside. The Carew family held their Pembrokeshire castle until Rhys ap Thomas acquired the property from Sir Edmund Carew, who was in serious financial straits late in the 15th century. Rhys subsequently became one of the region's most influential and celebrated leaders.

During the Wars of the Roses, Rhys ap Thomas initially sided with Yorkist Richard III, agreeing never to allow the king's rival, Harri Tudor, into Pembrokeshire. However, when Tudor landed in West Wales, Rhys actually joined the Lancastrian cause and fought at Bosworth Field. Upon Tudor's victory at Bosworth, the new king knighted Rhys ap Thomas and also created him chamberlain and justiciar of Wales. Even though Sir Rhys became an active member of King Henry VII's English court, his Welsh castle at Carew remained a favourite residence.

Sometime before the death of Arthur, the Prince of Wales, in 1502, Rhys revamped the castle, adding ornamentation that emphasised his ties to the monarchy, a residential level over the lesser hall and also the plain two storey outer gatehouse that visitors can examine today. Superficial alterations made to the great hall included an oriel window on the north side. Sir Rhys' most noteworthy contribution, however, was the grand porchway, which immediately attracts one's attention upon entering the inner ward.

Rhys ap Thomas' great porch

Over the entryway, he placed three skilfully carved heraldic emblems: the arms of King Henry VII flanked by the arms of his first son, Arthur, and his son's wife, Catherine of Aragon. Quite possibly, the crests were added to honour the marriage of Prince Arthur and Catherine of Aragon in 1501, for at this ceremony the Welshman's son, Gruffydd ap Rhys, received a knighthood for his service to the king. The attractive emblems have survived the ravages of the damp Welsh weather in remarkably fine condition.

In 1505, Rhys ap Thomas became a Knight of the Garter. The following year, Sir Rhys held the grandest tournament he could muster to honour his king. For five days, the participants, numbering well over 700 knights, their ladies and other nobility, retainers and servants gathered for what turned out to be an enormously successful celebration. Bedecked in the finest gilded armour, Rhys umpired the events. At his side were heralds and trumpeters, who announced each event and readied the knights. Contests included the joust, wrestling, tossing the pike, and swordplay. The tournament day was probably chaotic, with many events occurring simultaneously, but, despite the unavoidable drunkenness, no blood was shed.

In 1558, Sir John Perrot gained control of Carew Castle after the execution of Rhys ap Gruffydd, the grandson of Sir Rhys ap Thomas (see pp.32-34). The Perrot family owned several properties throughout Pembrokeshire, including Eastington and Haroldston (see separate entries), and Sir John became quite a powerful political figure, both in Pembrokeshire and abroad. Reputedly the illegitimate son of Henry VIII, Perrot had the talent for transforming castles into glamourous residences (he also owned Laugharne Castle in Carmarthenshire). Perrot's outspoken nature angered Elizabeth I, who ordered him thrown into the Tower of London. There, Sir John died of 'natural causes' before he could face execution.

During the 1580s, Sir John Perrot added Carew Castle's most distinguishing feature: the three-storey northern range of buildings, which overlooks the river through two rows of huge mullioned window frames and two large oriel windows. Now little more than a shell, the range replaced the older northern curtain wall and a tower at the north-eastern corner. The inner wall of this range

The northern range overlooking the river

retains the original outer wall of the northern curtain. Containing five rooms, Perrot's building completed the castle's transformation from military stronghold to lavish residence, and may have been built in anticipation of a visit from the queen. Stretching some 46 metres, a long gallery probably ran the entire length of the eastern two-thirds of the upper level, and, as at other stately homes, it may have housed the castle's art collection. There is some evidence that Perrot's castle contained lavish furnishings, a fine library and a collection of musical instruments. Apparently, Perrot never

Tudor gatehouse

completed the northern wing, for an inventory taken in 1592, shortly before his death, mentions a locked room which stored glass for the new building.

Historical records from the 16th century also document the existence of stables, a bakehouse, brewhouse, forge, and two walled deer parks on the surrounding Carew estates. Traces of these structures are now visible in the outer ward close to the ravelin built for the English Civil War (see below).

After Perrot's death, Carew Castle reverted to the Crown, and in 1597, Elizabeth granted the structure to her favourite, Robert Devereux, Earl of Essex. After she executed Devereux in 1601, Carew once again became Crown property. The Carew family finally regained rights to their Welsh castle in 1607, and may have installed glass into Perrot's northern range of buildings shortly thereafter. However, the rightful owner, Sir John Carew, was living at his wife's estate at Crowcombe in Somerset, England, and had little interest in this faraway piece of his inheritance. By 1611, Carew Castle had become derelict. Eight years later, Sir John Philipps, of nearby Picton Castle, leased the castle and lived there for a time.

The Philipps family initially held the castle for the Parliamentarian cause, but in 1642, a Royalist garrison was established at Carew by Lord Carbery. In 1644, Parliamentary forces led by Colonel Rowland Laugharne captured the castle and its garrison, but the Royalists regained control the following year. Shortly thereafter, Colonel Laugharne again assaulted the castle, which surrendered after almost a month-long siege, but not until the Parliamentarian forces had destroyed much of the southern range of buildings, which served to prevent reoccupation. The physical remains of this conflict survive on the grounds outside the main entrance, where archaeologists have unearthed the extensive remains of a Civil War defence, known as a ravelin, a V-shaped earthwork built to interfere with assaults on the flimsy outer gatehouse. Gun platforms have also been uncovered.

By 1687, the Carews had completely abandoned the structure, making their permanent residence in Somerset; however, their descendant, Anthony Trollope-Bellew, still owns the castle and its surrounding land. Since 1983, the family have leased the site to the Pembrokeshire Coast National Park Authority, who maintain the castle and open it to the public for a fee from March to November. Since 1984, besides the previously-mentioned Iron Age and Roman remains and artefacts, excavations have unearthed an early Norman bread oven and coins dating to the reign of King Stephen, the foundations of yet another gateway dating to the 13th century in the outer bailey, musket balls and pieces of the lead from the windows in Perrot's range, and a roadway built by Sir Rhys ap Thomas that led visitors toward his new gatehouse. Undoubtedly, much more awaits discovery at this magnificent historic monument.

Carew 'Rectory'

Tower house / fortified residence
Location: near Carew Cheriton church (SN 044 027)
Access: Exterior can be seen from public footpath

Park by the church and walk on down the lane, a footpath continuing through a small entrance gateway and onward through the grounds of the Rectory.

Incorporated into the later building now dubbed the 'Old Rectory', the medieval tower house is barely identifiable in the fabric of the post-medieval rectory. Probably dating to the 15th century, the history of this three-storey, battlemented square tower house is obscure. Historical documents possibly refer to the building as having a role in the English Civil War in 1645 when General Rowland Laugharne (then a Parliamentarian leader) moved through the area. Laugharne apparently encountered the garrison of his enemy at Carew, split up between two positions (probably the great castle and the 'old rectory'). As traces of the original entranceway indicate, the tower was originally accessed at first floor level and a spiral staircase inside the adjoining turret provided access to the upper level. At one time, a masonry wall may have enclosed the tower house, but it no longer survives.

Carswell

Tower House
Location: 2 miles west of Tenby (SN 098 010)
Access: Maintained by Cadw, and access is therefore allowed
but it stands on private ground

Park near the bridge over the stream on the road heading south-westwards out of St Florence towards Tenby. Here a public bridleway heads almost due west along the southern side of the stream. Take this and cross the lane that serves Tarr farms. After about another quarter of a mile the bridleway joins a farm access road, which you stay on when the bridleway veers off half right. When you reach Carswell Farm the tower house is located about two-thirds of the way along the western run of farm buildings.

Engulfed by a complex of farm buildings about two miles west of Tenby, Carswell is a fascinating example of what has been termed a yeoman's dwelling, one of several that dotted Pembrokeshire in the late Middle Ages. While little more than a two-storey stone house, Carswell (whose name derives from the Welsh, *gors* or 'marsh') did have some defensible features, including access at first floor level via a removable ladder and siting on a promontory overlooking the Ritec.

Just 5 metres square, Carswell was a humble yet functional home, consisting of a single domestic chamber on the first floor above a vaulted undercroft which held the kitchen and its enormous fireplace. The exterior is dominated by a massive square chimney, which is in excellent condition and has a small bread oven, a later addition, on one side. A large doorway on the northern side gave access only to the undercroft, which was lit by two slit windows, one of which is blocked. The room above probably acted as a solar or small private apartment. It too was fitted with a fireplace, and had four narrow windows set deep into embrasures. Unfortunately, much of this upper level no longer survives to allow a complete impression of the site, but the structural remains suggest that, for a time, the owners divided the chamber into two rooms. The roof was pitched and probably made of timber. The stone fireplace hood is the room's notable feature.

Although the oldest remains at the site date to the 16th century, Carswell probably was occupied by the early 14th century when it formed part of the estates of the earls of Pembroke. The earliest known occupant was William Wyte, who lived there in 1397. The site is mentioned in 16th-century records, during which the property was apparently held by two owners, Richard Merydith, who sold his house and hillside garden to Peter Williams, and the mayor, burgesses and bailiffs of Tenby. In 1543, Philip Nicholl owned the tower house. The Corporation of Tenby leased the site in the early 1600s to Thomas Bowen of Trefloyne, and then in 1689 sold portions of it to various local residents to raise money for poor relief. From then until 1960, when its tenants purchased the farm, ownership of Carswell was shared between the trustees of the Tenby Charities and the rector of St Mary's Church, also in Tenby. In 1982, Mr. and Mrs. B. Thomas placed the site in the care of the State and it is now managed by Cadw.

Another, similar late medieval building stands on the same property, however, it is not open to the public. Carswell is closely associated with West Tarr (see separate entry).

Castell Crychydd / Heron's Castle

> Motte / ringwork
> Location: 8¹/₂ miles south-east of Cardigan (SN 261 348)
> Access: Can be seen from adjacent road

Take the minor road that heads east-north-east from its junction with the A478 just north of Crymych. At Bwlchygroes, turn right, pass through Star and at the crossroads about a mile further on, turn left towards Llwyndrain. In Llwyndrain itself about a mile from the crossroads, take the first left, keeping left at the junction you immediately reach. Just beyond the farm at the brow of the hill on this road, the castle can be seen to the right (the far mound in the photograph). Take a good OS map as well!

The large earthen mound rises 5 metres and stretches some nine metres across the summit, which dips noticeably in the centre. This depression may indicate that the castle was actually a ringwork, however CARN, the site database of the of the Royal Commission on the Ancient and Historical Monuments of Wales (RCAHMW), characterise it as a motte. Remnants of what may have been a stone tower and a masonry wall survive on the summit. The associated oval-shaped bailey is identifiable, and measures 27 metres by 8 metres. Sections of the moat are also visible. The actual date of the site is uncertain, but it was probably standing at least by the late 12th century.

Castell Fartin / Ma(e)norowen

Ringwork / Motte
Location: About half a mile south of Goodwick (SM 943 368)
Access: None, on private ground not reached by footpath

Located on the end of the ridge that also holds Manorowen Woods, lie the scanty remains of a damaged motte or ringwork. Identified on early OS maps as 'earthwork', the overgrown site features an oval platform measuring about 3 metres. Its landward defences no longer survive.

Castell Llainfawr

Ringwork
Location: 1 mile south-east of Eglwyswrw (SN 151 374)
Access: Site is by-passed by footpaths, but nothing easily seen

Located about one mile south-east of Eglwyswrw (see separate entry), this site is difficult to locate. Take the B4332 south-easterly from Eglwyswrw and take the lane to the right after about a quarter of a mile. Watch for the second public footpath on your left (and which leads off almost opposite a farm track that heads off to the right). The footpath leads you towards Llainfawr farmhouse, the castle site being a few hundred yards to the south of the farm on the east side of the stream. Take a good OS map!

The remains of a modest ringwork and ditch are reported to still survive in marshy land at a bend in a tiny stream. The embankment measures almost 3 metres high. CARN, the site database of the RCAHMW identifies the site as a motte, but other sources (including the latest OS map) indicate otherwise.

Castell Pengawsai / Castell Blaenllechog

Ringwork
Location: 1¹/₂ miles east of Maenclochog (SN 110 280)
Access: Can be seen at a distance from the Bridleway to the east

To reach the site, take the minor road heading north-east from Maenclochog to Rhosfach. Just before the crossroads at Rhosfach a bridleway heads south, with a jink to the right and then left, to pass a farm over on the right. To the rear of the farm the ringwork may be made out.

The earthwork castle known as Pengawsai has been identified both as a small motte and as a small ringwork. The depression on the summit indicates the latter characterisation may be more accurate. Little survives of the enclosing ditch, but the ramparts remain fairly strong and still rise over 3 metres high. CARN, the site database of the RCAHMW has also documented the site as a possible hillfort.

Castell Pen Yr Allt

Ringwork
Location: 3 miles south-west of Cardigan (SN 158 420)
Access: Private, ask for permission at the farm at Llantood

Located on a ridge just north-east of tiny Llantood just off the A487 as it swings northwards toward Cardigan, the earthworks of Castell Pen yr Allt have been classified as a ringwork, a defended enclosure and a hillfort. Although seriously degraded by ploughing and quarrying, the site is presently identifiable. Still enclosed by a ditch, the banks of the ringwork rise some 5.7 metres on the southern edge, which slopes steeply and drops abruptly to the stream near its base. Stonework possibly from a masonry tower still litters the interior of the ringwork. The castle is invisible from the road or the footpath that passes by in the valley below.

Castell Poeth

Possible ringwork
Location: 3 miles west of Goodwick (SM 897 377)
Access: Visible from nearby roads

Located on the northern side of a V-junction, just behind a house, south-west of Harmony and 3 miles due west of Goodwick, Castell Poeth features a hugely overgrown circular bank and ditch measuring about 30 metres across. Another bank to the north-east may represent the limits of the outer bailey. CARN, the site database of the RCAHMW classifies the site as a ringwork, an Iron Age fort, a motte, or even round barrow.

Castlebythe

Motte
Location: In Castlebythe, 8 miles south-east of Fishguard (SN 021 290)
Access: Visible from road

Take the minor road from Tufton on the B4329 to the west and Castlebythe. Easy to find in the village, the motte is somewhat obscured by trees and other vegetation. Rising as much as 6 metres high, the squat motte has a summit stretching about 12 metres across. The original ditch has been in-filled, partly by the road that swings through the village and passes immediately alongside the motte. An oval bailey measuring 70 metres by 50 metres and enclosed with banks rising 3.5 metres high apparently once also existed here, but has long since been destroyed.

Castlemartin

Ringwork
Location: In Castlemartin, 4 miles south-west of Pembroke
(SR 915 984)
Access: Visible from nearby roads

As one attempts to negotiate the roundabout (an 18th-century cattle pound) in the compact village, it can be easy to bypass the remains of Castle Martin. Partially visible from the B4313, the large ringwork and bailey are located more or less opposite the military gate onto the Castlemartin Range.

The surprisingly extensive site measures 76 metres across. It features the well-preserved remains of the ring-bank and some remnants of the outer ditch. Modern buildings now stand in parts of the bailey, and field boundaries have impinged on a portion of the structure. Some speculation exists that the site may have originated as an Iron Age fort, of which there are several on the Castlemartin Peninsula. Recorded as early as the 13th century as *Castro Martini*, Leland described the castle in the 16th century as 'vestiges of Martin Castle'. Earthwork platforms and sunken lanes have been identified just beyond the current boundaries of the village, indicating that, besides the castle and medieval church, a medieval settlement once existed here.

Castlemorris

Now vanished possible motte
Location: (SN 903 316)

The placename suggests a castle once stood in the hamlet, which now only consists of a few farm buildings and houses. Maurice FitzGerald, one of Strongbow's (Richard de Clare's) knights, is believed to have erected the earthwork castle (reputedly a motte) that once stood here in the mid- to late 12th century. The castle was mentioned in the *Black Book of St Davids*, written in the mid-14th century. Castlemorris itself is located along the B4331, just east of Mathry.

Castle Pill (Blackbridge)

Ringwork
Location: Just east of Milford Haven (SM 918 064)
Access: Via footpath from the edge of Milford Haven

Take the footpath that leaves the A4796 just opposite Skomer Drive where there is a small park as the A road enters Milford Haven. Walk along the path until it joins a tarmacced lane, when the ringwork is seen directly ahead.

Variously listed as a ringwork, motte and hillfort, the mound near Milford Haven known as Castle Pill has not been treated with dignity over the centuries. The structure was partly destroyed in 1643 when Royalist troops built an artillery fort nearby to contain Parliamentary forces and is presently being damaged by tipping. Located on a craggy ridge at the junction of two streams, the oval enclosure consisted of a bank and ditch, and was most likely a ringwork. The earthworks still rise three metres and the remains of a stone revetment survive in places. Remnants of a D-shaped stone tower also survive.

Cilgerran

Enclosure Castle
Location: 3 miles south-east of Cardigan (SN 195 431)
Access: In the care of Cadw and open to the public

The fine stone castle is barely contained just north of the main village road, just east of the A478 from Cardigan, where parking can be something of a challenge.

Even though Cilgerran is only about three miles south-east of Cardigan, which is in Ceredigion, the village actually became part of Pembrokeshire when Henry VIII's Act of Union formally established the county. From the 12th to the 16th century, the lordship of Cilgerran formed part of the earldom of Pembroke.

Quite possibly originating as a ringwork, Cilgerran Castle commands a promontory site underlain with slate. The castle overlooks the steep-sided gorge cut by the River Teifi on the north and the rushing waters of the Plysgog, which scarped the sloping hills on the western side of the site. While nothing remains to verify that a ringwork did stand on the northern side of the promontory, it seems reasonable to conclude that the inner ward, which is separated from the outer ward by a natural fracture in the bedrock, may have been the site of the earliest stronghold at Cilgerran. The fracture was modified into an imposing ditch, which was later revetted with stone.

Early documents mention the existence of a castle complete with a ditch and wall called Cenarth Bychan, located in the cantref of Emlyn. The stronghold was apparently built in about 1108 by Gerald de Windsor, constable of Pembroke and Carew Castles (see separate entries), but no longer survives, with the possible exception of two lengths of stone walling held together with clay that may have afforded some strength to the earthen ramparts. One fragment can be seen on the western side of the inner gatehouse (added in the 13th century), and the second fragment is located about midway along the northern side of the inner ward.

There is a possibility that Gerald's earth and timber fortress was attacked and taken by Owain ap Cadwgan, Prince of Powys, only a year after its construction. But if this was the case, the Normans evidently quickly regained control of Cenarth Bychan and continued to hold it until 1165, when the Welsh, under the leadership of Rhys ap Gruffydd, Prince of Deheubarth, seized Cilgerran Castle and Nest's son, Robert FitzStephen. Even though the Normans assaulted Cilgerran twice during the next year, they were unable to recapture the castle. The Lord Rhys, as Rhys ap Gruffydd is better known, continued to control Cilgerran Castle until his death in 1197. Rhys's sons fought amongst themselves for control of Deheubarth and its castles, and by 1204 Welsh leadership in the region had become so disorganised that the Normans, led by William Marshal, Earl of Pembroke, recaptured Cilgerran Castle. However, in 1215, during Llywelyn ab Iorwerth's campaign against the Normans waged throughout much of Wales, the Welsh again took Cilgerran Castle, then probably still only defended with timber palisades and earthen embankments. It was another eight years before William Marshal II (the Younger) gathered a strong enough army to march on the Welsh and wrest the castle (and others) from their control.

In 1223, Marshal began Cilgerran's transformation from a modest earth and timber fortress into a substantial masonry castle, endeavouring to never again forfeit the site to the Welsh. The Marshals constructed a durable castle with two baileys, enclosed by a curtain wall and dominated by two massive round towers. In many ways, the finished product resembled their formidable castle at Pembroke (see separate entry). Today, most of what survives at Cilgerran Castle dates to this period, when the Marshals were earls of Pembroke. Even though the Welsh assaulted the site once more in 1257, they never again controlled the stronghold.

William Marshal II was probably responsible for enclosing the outer ward with a stone wall, which initially granted access to the castle from a simple gatehouse on the south-eastern side of the bailey. A ditch probably lined the exterior of this wall, but it has long since been in-filled and replaced with the lane and gardens that now rim the site. The only surviving section of that curtain wall stands at the eastern end of the inner ditch, which abuts the round tower. Originally battlemented, it now rises only to wall-walk level, the uppermost level having collapsed in the late 19th century. At the wall's base, a squarish sally port once allowed inhabitants to rush forth to attack unsuspecting enemies approaching outside the walls (see photograph at the start of this entry).

Remnants of the south-eastern gatehouse, which measured about 8 by 5 metres and contained a small guardroom on the eastern side, are visible alongside the foundations of a later, three-roomed

Drawbridge abutments fronting the inner gatehouse

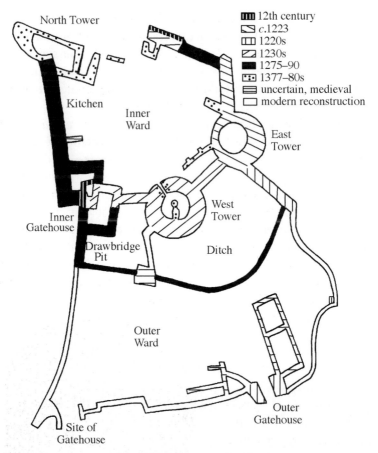

Legend:
- ▥ 12th century
- ◹ *c*.1223
- ⊞ 1220s
- ◩ 1230s
- ■ 1275–90
- ⚏ 1377–80s
- ≡ uncertain, medieval
- ☐ modern reconstruction

North Tower

Kitchen

Inner
Ward

East
Tower

Inner
Gatehouse

West
Tower

Drawbridge
Pit

Ditch

Outer
Ward

Outer
Gatehouse

Site of
Gatehouse

Plan of Cilgerran Castle

structure which projects into the outer bailey. (The outer bailey
itself measures an average of 27 metres across.) Fitted with a kiln
or oven, the function of the ruined building remains uncertain.
Blocked when the main entrance was moved to the western side of
the castle, the south-eastern gatehouse was probably defended by
double timber doors; no evidence exists that a portcullis was used
in this structure. Remnants of another, possibly later, gatehouse
were only recently discovered on the site of the modern entrance
into the castle.

Besides strengthening the outer bailey, William Marshal II also
made substantial changes to the inner ward, transforming the rela-

tively simple castle into a well-defended fortress with the construction of two powerful round towers. Marshal's east tower rose four storeys. A fairly simple building accessed at ground level, it contained a spiral staircase which linked the upper floors, but the only means of reaching the first storey from the ground floor was via a movable stairway that reached the trapdoor in the ceiling. A doorway on the second storey offered access to the adjoining wall-walk, which stretched northward from the tower to reach a set of latrine chutes which emptied into the gorge below. Only one fireplace served this tower from its isolated position on the uppermost level. Arrowslits faced the outer bailey, whilst two-light windows with seats overlooked the inner bailey.

Embedded in the curtain wall between the east and west towers, an arched postern gateway defended with a portcullis opened onto a short platform that faced the ditch and the outer bailey. Perhaps Marshal intended the doorway as a convenient escape hatch in the event the inner gatehouse was breached.

Probably erected by Gilbert Marshal, as indicated by the evidence presented below, the slightly larger and more accommodating west tower probably served as the castle's keep, replacing the east tower, which had formerly performed that role. The placement of the west tower astride the rock-cut ditch also suggests that it was built later than its sibling to the east. As with many other Norman keeps, the four-storey high west tower was accessed at first floor level by a wooden staircase; another entrance was cut into the wall at

West Tower

81

ground level, probably in the 14th century during the final building phase. Other features of note include a spiral staircase, a second storey fireplace, single-light windows facing the inner ward, and simple arrowslits opening towards the outer ward.

Gilbert Marshal's other contribution of note at Cilgerran was the inner gatehouse, which once stood three storeys high. To gain access to the inner ward, all visitors crossed a drawbridge which spanned the ditch. Its medieval abutments are visible beneath the modern footbridge. Today, only the inner gatehouse's arched entrance survives. Drawbar holes indicate that the gate passage was defended by a set of heavy timber doors. Portcullis grooves and the remains of what may have been a piscina suggest that the first floor of the inner gatehouse may have held the chapel as well as the mechanism for raising and lowering the iron grate. Immediately to the east of the archway, the cross-wall (equipped with arrowslits) rises higher than the ruins; it once linked the gatehouse to the upper levels of the west tower.

Changes in the construction of the cross-wall indicate a later date for the western tower and the gatehouse than for the east tower. The wall reputedly linked the east tower to a now vanished gate-house which stood just east of the surviving gatehouse. Remnants of drawbridge abutments from this earlier structure are visible in the ditch. This drawbridge apparently linked the two baileys at the flat area just left of the west tower. Speculation that Gilbert Marshal was responsible for these additions seems reasonable, as Gilbert, who held the earldom of Pembroke from 1234 to his death in 1241, is known to have made changes to at least one other Marshal castle, Chepstow in south-east Wales.

Marshal ownership of Cilgerran Castle ended with the death of the last male heir, Anselm, in 1245. Their vast estates were divided among William Marshal's daughters, and Eva, the widow of William de Braose, Lord of Abergavenny, inherited Cilgerran Castle. The castle passed by right of marriage from their daughter, another Eva, to her husband, William de Cantelupe. In the late 13th century, Cantelupe's nephew, John de Hastings, then in his minority, acquired ownership of the castle. Consequently, Cilgerran was placed in the hands of royal custodians, first passed to Prince

Edward (soon to become King Edward I) and then Prince Edmund, Henry III's second son. Neither of the Plantagenet princes spent much time nor money on this castle, their attention diverted to concerns elsewhere in the realm. Not surprisingly, the once formidable fortress began to decay. In 1275, records report that money was allocated for repairs and it was probably at this time that the curtain wall surrounding the inner ward was strengthened and a postern gate added along the wall on the south-western side, close to where the kitchen block stood.

The final building phase at Cilgerran Castle occurred in the 1370s. By this time, the new de Hastings heir was in his minority and the castle had again fallen into disrepair. However, the stronghold still had enough strategic value to the monarchy that King Edward III ordered repairs so that it could withstand an assault from the French, with whom England was at war. Besides adding several buildings to the inner ward, the foundations of which are still scattered around the bailey, modifications were made to the great round towers, and a new tower was constructed on the north-western corner of the inner bailey. The D-shaped north tower is now almost completely ruined, but in the 14th century it would have been well positioned to watch the activity on the Teifi and Plysgog waterways below.

After John de Hastings, the last male heir of that name, died in 1389, Cilgerran Castle and the lordship reverted to the Crown. Despite neighbouring Cardigan and other castles remaining active in the region's history, little else of consequence occurred at Cilgerran. In the late 15th century, William Vaughan managed the castle on behalf of King Henry VII, but Henry VIII abolished the lordship when he created the county of Pembrokeshire in the Act of Union.

By the early 18th century Cilgerran Castle was a ruin, and in the 19th century, portions collapsed due to quarrying. In 1938, the then owner, Sir Lewes Pryse, turned the site over to the National Trust, which passed control and consolidation work on to the State. Cilgerran Castle is now maintained by Cadw, and open to the public for a fee throughout the year.

Cresswell

Fortified residence
Location: 2 miles north of Carew (SN 049 070)
Access: Seen from nearby road

Best views are had from atop the narrow bridge that crosses the River Cresswell. This is reached by taking the minor road heading west at Cresselly. At the T-junction turn right (north). The site is located on the western side of the lane.

Peeking through the woodland, the greying remnants of Cresswell Castle still overlook the river. Built in the 16th century by William Barlow, Bishop of St Davids, the weakly defended structure was in reality a sham rather than a true castle. The bishop's own status as a powerful leader was emphasised with this structure, which consisted of a castellated rectangular enclosure and four corner towers, one of which held the dovecote. There is some speculation that the castle originated, possibly as early as the 13th century, as a stronghold intended to watch over the activity on the nearby river. Cresswell Castle was held by the Barlows until the late 17th century when they moved to more luxurious accommodation at Lawrenny. Afterwards, it was neglected and fell into decay.

Dale

Enclosure castle
Location: To the west of Dale on St Anne's Head (SN 806 059)
Access: Visible from public footpath

To view the sham castle, only possible from a distance, take the first minor lane heading west towards the parish church of St James shortly after entering the northern side of Dale via the B4327. A public footpath heads west towards the castle at the point where the lane turns south.

The 'castle' visible is in reality a sham, but may stand on the site of the original earthwork castle that reputedly stood here during the Middle Ages. CARN, the site database of the RCAHMW certainly documents the existence of an earthwork castle at the site, but it is no longer visible and may possibly have been incorporated into the later stone structure. This takes its name from the de Vale family, who owned the manor of Dale as early as the 12th century and were tenants of the barony of Walwyn's Castle (see separate entry). In 1293, Robert de Vale received a charter allowing him to hold a market and annual fair on the feast of St Crucis, which occurs each September 14th. Upon Robert's death ten years later, the de Vale estates were divided up among his four daughters, and in 1601, William Walter of Roch Castle (see separate entry) purchased a portion of the lordship of Dale, which then passed to his descendants. (Lucy Walter has the ignoble reputation of having been the mistress of Charles II and bearing the king's illegitimate son, who later became the Duke of Monmouth.)

Richard Walter sold the estate to David Paynter in 1669. Paynter's daughter carried the castle by right of marriage to William Allen of Gelliswick, and the Allens in turn passed the castle to the John Lloyds of Ffosybleiddiaid and Mabws in 1776. They assumed the surname Lloyd-Philipps in 1823 and made some alterations to the castle site, which produced the battlemented structure that we see today.

Dingstopple

Motte
Location: Half a mile north-west of Llawhaden (SN 061 186)
Access: None, and not visible from minor road

This tiny, tree-topped motte is situated off a minor road running south-west / north-east near Llawhaden, where the remains of an impressive bishop's castle are open to the public (see separate entry). The mound rises only 1.6 metres high and the summit stretches almost 9 metres across. A marshy ditch surrounds the motte, which is located at the head of a stream.

Drim

Ringwork
Location: 1 mile north-west of Llawhaden (SN 064 197)
Access: Public footpath passes close by

From Broadway, under 1 mile due north of Llawhaden, take the lane north, bearing left at the first road junction. Park where you can when you reach the pubic footpath/farm track just over the brow of the hill. Walk down the footpath heading to the left (west) and in about half a mile you'll reach Drim Farm. As you reach the farm buildings, take the footpath to the right and the castle is quickly reached on the ridge to your right.

On the northern side of Drim Farm, the remains of a much mutilated ringwork and ditch provide extensive views to the north.

(A much mutilated second earthwork that lies on another footpath heading south-west from Drim Farm is a defended enclosure, identified in CARN, the site database of the RCAHMW, as a hillfort or settlement.)

Dyffryn Mawr / Parc y Domen

Motte / ringwork
Location: 1 mile north-west of Crymych (SN 175 353)
Access: Can be seen from nearby footpath

In Crymych on the A478 Cardigan-Tenby road, take the minor road that heads north-west from by the pub. After a bit over half a mile, once the road has crossed a stream and starts to rise up hill, taking care, park at the entrance to a lane off to the right on a bend, the lane also being a public footpath. Walk along this and in a very short time the castle mound will be seen off to the right on the far side of the stream.

Some debate exists over the exact nature of this earthwork site. The Royal Commission and Ordnance Survey map record the site as a motte, however, others claim it is a small ringwork castle. Set on a gentle north-facing slope above streams to the east and west, the prominent tree-clad mound stands about 6 metres high, its scooped summit ranging 18 metres across. On the top are the possible remains of a stone wall, once held together with clay or poor quality mortar. The moat is fairly well preserved. Excavations in the early 20th century evidently uncovered traces of two post holes outside the wall itself.

88

Eastington / Jestynton

Fortified Residence
Location: West of Roscrowther, itself west of Pembroke Dock
(SN 901 024)
Access: Private, no access

Attached to a later structure and now located well off the beaten track down a lengthy private farm lane not too far from the medieval church at Rhoscrowther, the fortified residence once called Jestynton dates to the late 13th or early 14th century, when the ubiquitous Perrot family owned the site. The site takes its name from Jestyn (or Iestyn) ab Owain, who apparently settled here in the 10th century. In the 11th century, Sir Stephen Perrot may have acquired the property by right of marriage to Eleanor, Jestyn's great-granddaughter, although historian Roger Turvey has recently offered a convincing argument that Sir Stephen never actually existed.

By whatever means, the Perrots occupied the battlemented hall house-cum-tower house until the 16th century, when they moved to more luxurious accommodation near Haverfordwest (see entry on Haroldston). At the end of the century, they relinquished Eastington to the Philipps family when Sir John Perrot was charged with treason. However, it was not until the Meres (Meares) acquired the estate that any significant alterations were made to the original structure. They built a new farmhouse on the eastern side of the hall house, and probably also added a secondary domestic structure to the western façade. The Meres family continued to occupy Eastington until 1842, when they sold the farm to John Mirehouse, a major landowner on the Castlemartin Peninsula.

The fortified residence at Eastington, probably built by Peter Perrot, was a typical first floor hall house, of which many stood in medieval Pembrokeshire. The rectangular building measured about 13 by 7.5 metres and rose almost 8 metres high to reach the wall-walk. Access was at first floor level, initially via a movable ladder and later using a set of stairs, remnants of which still front the western side of the structure. Close by, a secondary building, perhaps housing a solar and another hall-block, also stood. Unfortunately, only traces of that building survive. The hall house itself consisted of a barrel vaulted undercroft with three arrowslits at ground level, and a single large chamber equipped with fireplace, trefoil-headed windows and a latrine chute on the floor above. The roofline was rimmed with a substantial set of battlements and a wall-walk.

The remains of the fortified residence at Eastington are visible from afar. Situated on property owned by the neighbouring Texaco refinery, which purchased the site in 1957, access to the medieval site is restricted. Sadly, the Perrots' two storey manor house at Popton was demolished to make way for the refinery. The Edwards family continues to lease the site at Eastington, and farm the property as they have done for over 100 years. To reach Eastington itself, park near the outer end of the narrow lane that leads onto the farm and walk towards the site. The lane itself is located just north of the church, near where the main road curves eastward past the refinery site. The fortified residence is visible from the lane's end.

Eglwyswrw

Ringwork
Location: On the western end of the village (SN 139 384)
Access: Questionable path goes onto the site

Signs suggest visitors can pass through the gate to the village's sewage works at the western end of the village, to the north of the A487. The castle lies above this track and is approached by what looks to be a well worn short footpath.

The prominent ringwork and bailey earthworks measures about 18 metres by 27 metres, and rises about 2.5 metres on its south-western side. Both the southern and western sides retain their banks and ditches. The northern defences were formed by naturally steep slopes. Masonry remains from what may have been a square tower can be seen at one corner (see photo above), and more stonework probably exists under the rubble of the collapsed walls.

The ringwork at Eglwyswrw may have been the original manorial seat of the Cantington family, who later moved to Court Farm, a moated site about half a mile north-west of the castle.

Glyn Patel / Green Castle / Crinow

Motte
Location: 1 mile east of Narberth (SN 128 142)
Access: Site just about visible from nearby road junction

Located on farmland south-east of tiny Crinow, just off the B4314 not too far east of Narberth, this small motte rises about 4.5 metres and stretches 9 metres across the summit. A bailey may have existed to the north-west of the motte. It is just about visible from the junction of the B4314 with the minor road to Lampeter Velfrey.

Along with the earthwork castle at nearby Lampeter Velfrey (see separate entry), this motte belonged to the commote (*cwmwd*) of Efelffre, which was incorporated into the lordship of Narberth in the 13th century. During the 11th and 12th centuries, Efelffre was under the control of William FitzBaldwin and his descendants, and for a time was part of the lordship of St Clears. In 1171, King Henry II granted Efelffre to Rhys ap Gruffydd, and in the late 13th century it was merged with the earldom of Pembroke.

Haroldston

Fortified residence with Tower House
Location: Immediately south of Haverfordwest (SN 958 145)
Access: Visible from adjacent public footpath

To reach Haroldston, take the A4076 southward around Haverfordwest to the roundabout at Merlin's Bridge. Turn left onto the first exit, which heads into the village, and having passed under the railway bridge turn left onto St. Issell's Avenue and continue along the lane beyond the school. The remains are on the left hand side, just after a public footpath sign off to the left and before a lane with a no through road sign off to the right. There is a wide area where you can park between these two points. Then take the footpath. Site tours and lectures on the history of the house and the families who lived there are regularly offered by Roger Turvey, an expert on the Perrot family in Pembrokeshire, by prior arrangement with the Guild of Freemen.

Overlooking the A4076, on a truncated hillside opposite Priory Hill on the eastern side of Haverfordwest, sit the extensive remains of Haroldston, the former seat of the Perrots, one of Pembrokeshire's most influential medieval and Elizabethan families. Though the origins of the manor's name may be traced to Viking times, it is more likely that the name comes from 14th-century owners, whose surname was Harold (Harald). By 1301, Sir William Harold had been appointed as constable of Haverfordwest Castle, and his family continued to play an active role in local and national politics. They became stewards to the lord of Haverford, and held the manor until the late 14th century, when the heiress, Alice, inherited Haroldston and its estates. The property in turn passed by right of marriage to Peter Perrot, whose family occupied Eastington (see separate entry), a fortified residence still standing on the Castlemartin Peninsula. The Perrots held Haroldston from 1442 until the last heiress, Hester Perrot, married Sir John Packington of Worcester in about 1700 and moved away. Afterwards, the site was leased to various tenants, who allowed it to decay.

One of the area's greatest benefactors, Sir John Perrot, was born at Haroldston in November 1527. Besides being something of a dandy who transformed the castles at Carew (see separate entry) and Laugharne in Carmarthenshire into palatial residences, Perrot was reputedly Queen Elizabeth I's half-brother. For some time, historians have believed that Henry VIII had had a liaison with Mary Berkeley, a lady-in-waiting to the royal household and the wife of Sir Thomas Perrot, and that baby John was the result. However, Roger Turvey, an expert on the life and times of Sir John Perrot, has suggested that this tradition has no factual basis (see also pp.31-34).

During Sir John's controversial career, he became Mayor of Haverfordwest, Lord Lieutenant of Pembrokeshire, Lord Deputy of Ireland, a Member of Parliament, member of the Queen's Privy Council, and Vice-Admiral of the Fleet. Ultimately, he suffered the fate of so many political leaders during the Tudor Dynasty and died in the Tower of London in 1592, while awaiting execution for treason. In his will, Perrot endowed the town of Haverfordwest with a great financial legacy, which is still operated as the Sir John Perrot Trust. The Trust still owns several dwelling-houses in the town and the fine row of 12 almshouses along Perrot's Terrace.

Probably originating as a first floor hall, Haroldston became one of Pembrokeshire's finest residences. Today, it is extensively ruined and in danger of completely disappearing if not promptly consolidated. Once surrounded by walled gardens, a pleasuance, several groves of trees, and even a hops garden, the site must have been quite impressive in its heyday. Sadly, most of the structure is overgrown or tumble-down, chunks of masonry seemingly strewn around the site. Grass-covered walls outline the site and depressions in the land closest to the lane that passes the property signify the remains of gardens or, perhaps, fishponds. The historic site itself still extends to the edge of the hill overlooking the A4076. Humps in the fields indicate that ruins probably survive beneath the surface.

What survives of medieval Haroldston is difficult to identify; indeed, even historians are uncertain about the exact layout of the site which has never been fully excavated. Dominating the northern side of Haroldston is a thick length of walling (about one metre in width) which ends in the ruins of a substantial three-storey towered gatehouse, known as Steward's Tower. The gatehouse offered panoramic views of the rest of the site, and to the lands beyond. Remnants of the spiral staircase are visible and — with caution — can be used to reach the first floor of the gatetower. Inside, visitors will note a vaulted undercroft, the remains of fireplaces, latrine turrets, and small slits for lighting.

Immediately to the south of Steward's Tower stand the extensive remains of the first floor hall, which also featured a vaulted undercroft which now opens on the western side of the site. Lit at either end with two trefoil-headed lights, the hall was linked to the gatetower by an arched doorway. Most of the remaining masonry at Haroldston is little more than a jumble of walls and angular surfaces, the site apparently pilfered for building material after its final abandonment in the early 1800s. By 1811, the former pride of the Perrot family had become a complete ruin.

Haverfordwest

Enclosure Castle
Location: Haverfordwest (SN 953 157)
Access: Freely accessible

Wandering the narrow lanes and streets lining Haverfordwest's centre, one immediately experiences an affinity with its medieval past. The castle towers overhead, crowning a rocky knoll some 28 metres above the western branch of the River Cleddau. The river still cuts through Haverfordwest, but ships sailing from Milford Haven can no longer reach this far inland. Three medieval parish churches mark the skyline, while ageing buildings, shops and street names (and a few blue plaques) remember the past. It is as a planted borough that Haverfordwest achieved its success and the official status of a 'county in itself,' first by charter in 1479 and then reiterated by statute in 1543.

While the earliest records for settlement of this spot date to the 12th century, the presence of prehistoric tumuli, stone circles, standing stones and burial chambers lends credence to the notion that the area was known to Neolithic peoples, and probably to others even earlier. Reference to Ordnance Survey maps reveal prehistoric monuments near Uzmaston and Pelcomb Bridge, and on Great Treffgarne and Plumstone Mountains. But nothing substantial remains to give a prehistoric date to the town site that developed into medieval Haverfordwest.

Better evidence exists for Roman contact with the Celtic inhabitants of the area. For decades, some historians speculated that the Romano-British leader, Magnus Maximus (Macsen Wledig, in Welsh lore), had actually built a forerunner to the medieval castle, called Caer Alun, sometime in the 4th century AD. Historians have now discarded this notion, but recent findings based on aerial photos, artefacts and metal detector finds suggest that a Roman road once connected their fort at Carmarthen with Haverfordwest. For some time, the town museum displayed a small cache of Roman coins dating to the reigns of Valerianus, Gallienus, Postumus, Victorinus and Claudius Gothicus, reputedly found locally. Unfortunately, the coins have long since disappeared, but their existence supports the notion that the Romans reached this far west in Wales.

How Haverfordwest acquired its name remains clouded in uncertainty. Not adding the 'west' until the 15th century, the town has variously been called Haverford, Hareforde, Hafurdwest, Harfat, Hafart, Haverfordia, Averford, Haffort, Havreford, Hwllford (its Welsh name), Hawrfort, Hawrffordd, and Herefordensis in occidentali parte (on a 16th century warrant for the attainder of Sir John Perrot). Many scholars have suggested that the name derives from the Norse, *Havardr's fjorda* or *Hafna fiord*, meaning something akin to 'the haven of the frith,' a placename also appearing in Iceland. Most historians now favour a Saxon/Old English derivation, combining *haefer*—'he-goat or 'buck'—with 'ford', thereby implying that this was a spot where bucks could ford the river at its shallowest point.

Quite possibly, Haverford was amended to distinguish it from the cathedral town, Hereford, on the English border. Indeed, some documents refer to it as 'Herefordwest'. At least one historian has claimed that the 'west' was added, probably in the 14th century, by some bungling officials who persisted in confusing the Scandinavian Haverford with the Saxon Hereford. Perhaps a more plausible explanation is that the 'west' was added after Edward II granted Aymer de Valence, Earl of Pembroke, the town and castle of Hartford (now Hertford) to prevent any confusion from having possessions in towns with such similar names.

97

However the town actually received its name, Haverford became the unofficial capital of Little England Beyond Wales. As early as 1107, Henry I deliberately encouraged the Flemings to settle the lands to the west and south of the River Cleddau known as the Hundred of Rhos.

For years, the identity of the original castle-builder at Haverfordwest has been hotly debated, for a time settling on Gilbert de Clare, Earl of Pembroke, as the most likely candidate, even though there are no records to substantiate this claim. In fact, the earliest records referring to Haverford Castle date to the 12th century, when Gerald of Wales chronicled his journey through Wales. Recently, historians have come to accept that it was probably Tancred, a Fleming, who began Haverfordwest Castle in about 1110. Married to Gerald's aunt, Tancred (or Tancard) also had ties to the villages near Hayscastle called Upper and Lower Tancredston and Tancredston Bridge, still located about five miles north of Haverfordwest. Tancred's children intermarried with several local families. One of his daughters wed Gerald of Wales's brother, Philip de Barri, Lord of Manorbier (see separate entry). More than likely, therefore, it was the Flemings who were responsible for the first castle at Haverford, beginning construction shortly after their arrival in the area.

Tancred's castle at Haverford dominated the hilltop overlooking the Western Cleddau at the highest tidal point where ships could safely sail inland. The view commanded by the castle certainly explains the choice of its siting, as does its location just 140 metres from the river. The Fleming's castle would have featured earth and timber defences, which were eventually replaced with stone. The basic plan of the original castle is easy to identify in the current remains. The site also determined the future layout of the town. Initially, villagers probably lived in thatched huts on the hillsides close to the castle, while the wealthiest residents lived just beyond the castle walls. The layout of medieval Haverfordwest and its physical association with the castle are still quite evident in the plan of the present town.

Tancred's son, Richard FitzTancred, was an imposing figure who became the castle's constable in 1130 and also received the title of Lord of Haverford from Gilbert de Clare, Earl of Pembroke. In about 1135, the castle withstood the first of several Welsh assaults, this one led by Gruffydd ap Rhys, Prince of Deheubarth, who evidently captured the castle but lost it to the Normans shortly thereafter. According to Gerald of Wales, who visited Haverford with Archbishop Baldwin in 1188, FitzTancred was responsible for the care and education of three children, one of whom was de Clare's son and all of whom made a habit of visiting one of the castle's prisoners. They took pity on the man, who had a penchant for making arrows. The boys apparently received permission for the prisoner to visit their room, where-upon he grabbed an axe and threatened to kill his benefactors, unless he obtained 'indemnity and security ... in the most ample manner'.

Richard FitzTancred probably began the transformation of the original earth and timber fortress into stone in the late 12th century. The final creation was a combination of essentially two building periods, one initiated by FitzTancred in the late 12th century and a second begun in the late 1300s. Haverfordwest Castle essentially consists of two baileys: a rectilinear inner ward positioned on the eastern side of the hilltop and defended with corner towers and a large outer ward to the west. Now mainly used as a car park, the outer bailey is still partly enclosed by the 12th-century curtain wall and features remnants of a large square tower which stood along-side stables as early as 1387. The original entrance into the outer ward no longer exists, but during the Middle Ages, it probably consisted of a simple gatehouse and a drawbridge, which spanned the now in-filled ditch. Most of the castle's surviving masonry surrounds the inner bailey, which contained the main residential buildings, the well and the chapel.

More than likely, FitzTancred erected the castle's oldest surviving stone building—the three-storey structure which prob-ably served as the keep. At one time, it measured 13 metres long by 9 metres wide and had walls about 2.5 metres thick. Today, only the exterior walls survive to any substantial degree, facing north and curving east to overlook the River Cleddau. Arrowslits and vaulted walls are barely identifiable at ground level.

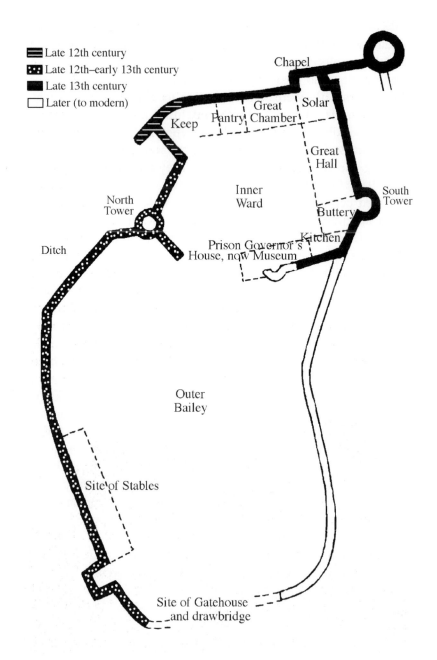

Late 12th century
Late 12th–early 13th century
Late 13th century
Later (to modern)

Chapel

Keep

Pantry

Great
Chamber

Solar

Great
Hall

North
Tower

Inner
Ward

South
Tower

Ditch

Buttery

Kitchen

Prison Governor's
House, now Museum

Outer
Bailey

Site of Stables

Site of Gatehouse
and drawbridge

Plan of Haverfordwest Castle

Known as the North Tower (and sometimes identified as the Brechinock Tower), the large round tower standing closer to the entrance into the inner ward was a well-defended structure that stretched about 8 metres in diameter and had walls some 2 metres thick offering access at first-floor level (like many Norman keeps). Overlooking the eastern end of the rock-cut ditch (4 metres wide by 2 metres deep) which fronted the northern side of the castle, the tower was probably built shortly after the completion of the keep, either by FitzTancred or his son, Robert FitzRichard, who may have completed the building works begun by his father. Alternatively, the Marshals may have done this construction work in the years immediately after King John granted them the castle in 1213.

By 1204, Robert FitzRichard (also known as Robert de Hwllford) controlled Haverford and its castle. Not only did Robert supply troops for King John's army, he was also responsible for extending the privileges of the town, and obtained the right to hold a Sunday market and an annual fair. Robert also established the Augustinian priory along the waterfront, now in ruins but recently excavated and consolidated and open to the public any reasonable time. John actually visited Haverford Castle on his way to and from Ireland in 1210, when FitzRichard still held the king's respect.

The North Tower

101

After suffering FitzRichard's bankruptcy, the disfavour of King John and death in 1211, the lordship and the castle of Haverford passed to William Marshal, Earl of Pembroke, after payment of a large sum of money. Over the course of the next three decades, Marshal and his sons granted the town six charters and initiated its transformation from a modest settlement into a borough, and then into a county in itself.

Gaining additional privileges with each succeeding charter granted by the Marshals during the 13th century, Haverford expanded physically as burgesses extended their real estate holdings and began constructing new houses. Soon, a small planted community had grown in the castle's shadow. Known as Castleton, or Castle Towne, the settlement was enclosed by a circuit of town walls, the bulk of which no longer survives. Entrance into the walled town was through one of four gates: Red Gate (the eastern gateway) sat at the end of Holloway, a covered lane that linked the castle to the river front; North Gate guarded the northernmost end of North Street; South Gate stood at the summit of Market Street, not too far from where St Thomas's was built; and, West Gate barred access on Dew Street, close to St Mary's Church. At first only one parish church, St Martin's, stood within the town walls, but by the 13th century St Mary's was also encompassed within Castleton. The third parish church, St Thomas's, remained just outside the walls. The two religious houses, the Augustinian priory (which had control of the parish churches) and the Dominican Friary, also remained beyond the town walls.

More than likely, the first town walls were built of timber; but, in 1263, when Humphrey de Bohun II, then Earl of Pembroke, granted the burgesses and officials of Haverford the right to levy murage, the borough walls were strengthened in stone. It was during this extension of the walls that St Mary's Church found itself inside Castleton. Today, virtually nothing remains of the town walls, except for bits that can be identified on the eastern side of Perrot's Road, close to the Wesleyan Chapel, and a short length just south of St Martin's Church, behind the houses at 34 and 35 Church Street.

A Welsh onslaught against the Normans reached Haverford in 1220, when Llywelyn ab Iorwerth (also called Llywelyn the Great)

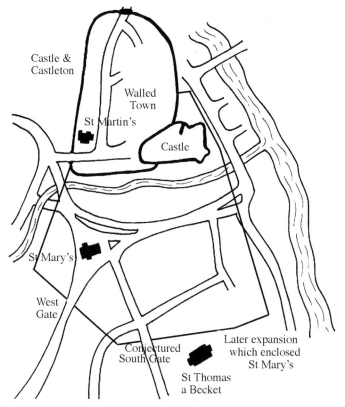

Plan of Haverfordwest

stormed Pembrokeshire and burned the town, right up to the castle gates. The castle proved worthy to the task, however, and the Welsh were forced to retreat. Reconstruction of the town proceeded rapidly. Upon the death in 1241 of Anselm, the last male heir to the Marshal earldom of Pembroke, the vast estates were divided among the five surviving female heiresses. The lordship and castle of Haverford ultimately passed to Humphrey and Eleanor de Bohun (William Marshal's granddaughter), and then to their son, Humphrey II, in 1248. In 1265, William de Valence, seized Haverford Castle from de Bohun, and was granted formal custody upon Humphrey's death later that same year. However, in 1274, Edward I returned control of the castle to the rightful de Bohun heir, Humphrey III.

103

By the end of the 13th century, Edward I had effectively quelled the Welsh rebellion against him, Llywelyn ap Gruffydd (the Last) was dead, and a new ring of mammoth castles dominated the northern reaches of Wales. In 1284, Edward and his queen, Eleanor of Castille, passed through Little England Beyond Wales on a pilgrimage to St David's and probably took great notice of the de Bohun castle. Five years later, Edward granted the lordship of Haverford and its castle to his queen, having himself acquired it from Humphrey de Bohun II in 1289. From then onwards, Haverford Castle remained a royal stronghold.

During the single year that Eleanor owned the castle (she died in 1290), she invested considerable money on repairing and maintaining the structure, paying over £800 for carpentry work and other expenses. Upon her death, William de Valence, Earl of Pembroke, regained custody of the castle and continued the queen's building works. Much of the surviving stonework probably dates to that time. Other women who held the castle and the lordship of Haverford were Isabelle, wife of Richard II, and Anne Boleyn, wife of Henry VIII, who governed the castle as Marchioness of Pembrokeshire.

Except for the foundations, the ruins enclosing the southern and eastern sides of the inner bailey date to the final building phase, which took place in the late 13th century and was the combined work of Queen Eleanor and William de Valence. The queen apparently decided to transform her new castle into something of a palace, and set about erecting two ranges of structures highlighted by huge windows to fulfil her lofty ambitions. Directly ahead as one enters the inner ward stand the remains of the eastern range, which rose two storeys and filled the entire length of the castle east of the keep. Alongside the keep, two garderobes with chutes emptied into a cesspit, which in turn dumped the waste outside the castle walls. A square chamber—identified by some as the pantry—adjoined the so-called great chamber, once lit by three large windows, now blocked. The chamber probably held private apartments and, perhaps, the queen's solar.

Along the southern side of the inner ward, Eleanor began the hall block, which also rose two levels. The great hall filled an area on the first floor measuring some 12.8 metres by 6 metres. Some historical records indicate that a 'coining house' occupied the ground floor level, but, as no coins have been found to confirm that a mint was located in the castle, it seems more likely that the vaulted basement, which contained four windows and a fireplace, served some administrative function. At the eastern end of the range, the South Tower provided access to upper levels and a garderobe, and to the neighbouring Queen's Arbour (or Queen's Bower), a terraced garden area outside the walls watched over by yet another round tower, which may have been linked to the main walls by a shorter wall. Today, the Queen's Arbour is a grassy hillside fitted with steps and a pathway which weaves its way towards the entrance to the outer ward.

The remains of a second round tower, known as the South (or Southwest) Tower, project outward from the south-facing side of the curtain wall. The present tower was probably added during the final building phase at the castle and may have replaced an earlier late 12th or early 13th century tower built at the same time as the North Tower. At the south-eastern corner of the inner ward, a rectangular tower sometimes called the South East Tower or the Buttress Tower once held the chapel, which was lit by a lancet window on the first floor. The tower, added during the initial building programme, was remodelled in the 19th century to accommodate the prison's treadmills.

Maintaining Haverford Castle was expensive, and, by 1308, when Aymer de Valence, Earl of Pembroke, governed the castle, the lead roofs leaked. According to the Pipe Rolls of 1326, two years after ownership had again reverted to the Crown due to the minority of the heir, wages for one janitor and one matchman were $1\frac{1}{2}$d. per day per man and a plumber received 12s. to repair defects in the castle lead. In 1404-5, repairs to the castle stable cost 18s., while construction of a new castle gate cost £3 3s. $6\frac{1}{2}$d. By then the janitor's fee had increased to 2d. per day, while the armourer received 13s. 4d. yearly.

By 1324, Haverford contained 360 burgages, making it one of Wales's largest medieval towns. Many medieval street names are still evident: Barn Street was Banstrete; Bridge Street was Brygestret; Dew Street was Deweystrete; Goat Street was

Gotestret; Quay Street was Ship Streate; Dark Street was Derkestret or Durkstret; Friars Lane was Frerestrete. A particularly interesting spot was known during the Middle Ages as Schytericheslake, Scyterich, Sittringlake or Shitters Lake. Located at the base of the castle on its southern side, a ravine of sorts was created by a small brook that flowed toward the River Cleddau. On either side, homes once surrounded the stream, and residents used it as a convenient sewer. Today, the houses no longer survive and the area has been in-filled. It now contains a large car park, equipped appropriately enough with a set of modern conveniences!

In 1343, Edward, the Black Prince, ordered a survey of Haverford Castle which reported that the masonry and lead-roofed castle was in fairly sound condition. His grandmother, the former Queen Isabella, the wife of Edward II also known as the 'she-wolf of France', actually owned the castle from 1331 to her death in 1358. Before 1374, Edward granted the already decaying structure to Thomas de Felton, continuing a long-standing pattern of owner-ship switching hands on a regular basis. Extensive and expensive repairs were made to the castle in 1381 around the time of Felton's death. Two years later, King Richard II granted the castle and lord-ship to John de Clanvowe, who died in 1391, and then to Thomas Percy, Earl of Worcester, who lost his head for treason in 1403 after his capture at the Battle of Shrewsbury.

During the Glyndwr Rebellion in 1405, an estimated 120 ships carrying as many as 3,000 French supporters of the Welsh freedom fighter advanced from Milford Haven to attack Haverford and its castle. The garrison managed to withstand the onslaught by the 800 men-at-arms, 600 crossbowmen and 1,200 foot soldiers, but the French slaughtered many townsfolk and destroyed Haverford by fire before heading to Tenby to join Glyndwr. Tenancy of Haverfordwest Castle continued to change hands frequently during the rest of the 15th century. Leases were granted to William de la Pole; Edward, Prince of Wales; Margaret of Anjou; Richard, Duke of York; William Herbert, Earl of Pembroke; Henry, Duke of Buckingham; and Jasper Tudor, Duke of Beaufort and uncle to Harri Tudor, the future King Henry VII, who was born in nearby Pembroke Castle (see separate entry).

In 1479, Edward IV granted a charter of incorporation to Haverfordwest which formally designated the borough as 'the county of the town of Haverfordwest' and authorised a new mayor, a sheriff and two bailiffs, and a 24-member common council. In 1500, administration of the town and castle passed as a fee-farm to the corporation, which paid the king an annual rent of £26 12s. 4^1/2d. Edward also approved the expenditure of £100 for castle repairs.

In 1543, Henry VIII signed the second Act of Union, which proclaimed that 'the town of Haverfordwest shall be a county in itself as it hath been before this time used, at the will and pleasure of the King's said Majesty, and that it shall be separated from the county of Pembroke at the King's said pleasure'. Unfortunately, Haverfordwest Castle declined so much during the reign of the Tudor monarchs that, by 1577, it was considered 'utterlie decayed'.

Nonetheless, Haverfordwest Castle was deemed strong enough to play a part in the English Civil War, initially in support of the Royalist cause. In 1643, the Parliamentarians seized the castle, but it continued to endure months of alternating alliances. In 1645, the Royalist garrison was resoundingly defeated at nearby Colby Moor, and Parliamentary forces gained permanent control of Haverfordwest Castle. In 1648, Cromwell's forces defeated the Royalists once and for all, and their leader ordered the corporation of Haverfordwest to slight the castle. The expense of the work led only to a partial demolition of the castle; however, portions of the site promptly became a quarry for building material.

In 1780, construction of a new county gaol was completed inside the grounds of Haverfordwest Castle, work that entailed the conversion of several of the medieval structures. Placed along the southern wall of the inner ward, the compact prison building measured 4 metres by 2 metres, had brick flooring and lead doors prevented escape. Among the most notable prisoners incarcerated in the early prison were French prisoners of war seized during the last invasion of Britain (near Fishguard) in 1797. In 1816, a debtors' prison was added along the wall between the North Tower and the attractive governor's house (now the town museum), which stands on the site of the original inner gatehouse. In 1820, an even larger, three-storey gaol was built in the outer ward of the castle, the remains of which are now occupied by the Pembrokeshire Record Office. In time, it held some 110 cells, a chapel and a small court house, and had eight wards with male and female work rooms, day rooms and airing yards. To keep the prisoners occupied in useful activities, two treadmills (one for men and the other for women) were installed inside the inner ward on the site of the medieval chapel to produce flour for their own bread.

After 1878, when the gaol was closed and prisoners sent to Carmarthen, the Pembrokeshire Police Force moved into the empty buildings. In 1963, many of the buildings were torn down, and the county museum occupied the main structure for a time. Then, the former gaol housed the town museum and county archives. In 1999, the museum moved into the neighbouring governor's house; the archives have remained in the larger building. Both are accessible to the public.

Hayscastle

> ### Motte
> Location: 7 miles north-west of Haverfordwest (SM 897 257)
> Access: Can be seen from adjacent road

In Hayscastle Cross on the B4330, take the road to the west sign-posted Roch. At the next crossroads turn left, and after about a mile, and past a road off to the right, the motte can be seen on the left, just before the entrance to Haycastle Farm.

Although mentioned in the *Black Book of St Davids* (1326), little else is documented about the site. Clearly visible if one is paying attention, the flat-topped oval motte is about 17 metres in diameter and 6 metres high. The summit of the mound is easily accessed, even through the underbrush, and is scattered with stone fragments (from a structure?). Heavily eroded on the north-western side, animals have burrowed tunnels into the mound from at least two directions. The ditch is partially wet on the north-western side, where it is closer to the road, and contains stone fragments on the north and eastern sides of the motte. A bailey probably existed to the east, but modern fencing prohibits access to that portion of the site.

Hean / Hen Castell

Motte
Location: One mile north of Saundersfoot (SN 138 059)
Access: Visible from nearby minor road

For some curious reason, this motte is not shown on most maps, but the castle is easily seen from the road to Wiseman's Bridge about one mile north of Saundersfoot. As the road climbs up the hill on which the house also called Hean Castle sits, there is a small lodge on the right with a 'private' sign. Just past this a lane leads off to the left and the castle mound is alongside and below this lane, not many yards from the junction.

Meaning 'Old Castle' in Welsh, the mound is overshadowed by the later mansion located just up the hill. At various times the entire estate has been owned by the Wogans, one of Pembrokeshire's most influential families, by the Lewis family, Barons Merthyr, and others. The tree-covered motte is in excellent condition.

Henry's Moat / Castell Hendre

Motte
Location: (SN 045 275)
Access: Visible from adjacent minor road

Henry's Moat is located at the southern end of the village of the same name on a minor road off to the south of the B4329.

This is a motte castle of which no history is known. Its name, Hendre, translates to 'old dwelling' or 'old town', which may indicate it was the predecessor of the motte castle at New Moat. Henry's Moat is 10.7 metres in diameter at the summit and its best preserved side (nearest the church) stands about 4.4 metres high. The ditch has been filled in and the mound has been extensively damaged by what appears to be private quarrying on the eastern side. The western side gradually ascends to the summit of the mound, while the north, south and east sides are fairly steep.

The circular motte is covered with a heavy growth of bracken and tall grasses. The castle is freely accessible on the southern side but a makeshift fence of barbed wire restricts access to the north and east areas of the mound. The eastern side is restricted due to the quarrying and the damage to the mound is clearly visible.

Lampeter Velfrey / Castell Cynon

Ringwork
Location: (SN 155 146)
Access: Visible from the road through the village

Located on a narrow ridge to the north of the church on the northern side of the village, portions of the earthwork banks of this prominent ringwork still rise over three metres and stretch about 36 metres across. A ditch fronts the site in parts. The overgrown structure has also been characterised as a motte, but this is incorrect.

Like nearby Glyn Patel, the earthwork castle at Lampeter Velfrey was part of the commote (cwmwd) of Efelffre. For more information, please refer to the separate entry on Glyn Patel.

Lamphey Palace

Bishop's Palace
Location: On the northern side of the village to the east of
Pembroke (SN 018 099)
Access: In the care of Cadw and open to the public

Presently, Lamphey Palace is maintained by Cadw, who open the site for a fee throughout the year. The palace is located north-east of the A4139 just opposite Lamphey Court.

The Bishops of St Davids had a vast number of holdings spread throughout Pembrokeshire. Besides their grandest palace alongside St Davids Cathedral, they also owned a fine residence in the manor of Lamphey, which they held as feudal lords. Today, the secluded ruins only hint at the medieval splendour of the site, for many of the buildings have long since disappeared. In its heyday, however, the rectangular compound with its inner and outer courtyards rimmed with all the buildings needed to manage an important manor would have been a stunning vision. The complex not only emphasised the status of the bishop but also offered him a comfortable place to live the good life.

The origins of the placename are speculative. However, many historians believe that Lamphey derives from Llandyfai or 'church of Tyfai'. Tyfai was the infant nephew of St Teilo, who established an Early Christian community at Penally, about 9 miles to the east. The church itself still dominates the centre of the village where the

A4139 bends and weaves as it heads west towards Pembroke and east towards Penally.

The structures presently comprising Lamphey Palace date mainly from the 13th to the 16th centuries. More than likely, timber buildings may have first occupied the site, but they no longer exist. In the very early 13th century, Gerald of Wales mentions the palace in a letter to Bishop Geoffrey de Henlaw when he complains that Henlaw's retinue should have been housed at his own manor at Lamphey rather than at three smaller, less equipped locations at Carew, Stackpole and Tenby and overburdening their monks. An early deed, dated to the mid-13th century, mentions the palace in association with Bishop Richard Carew. The extensively ruined 'Old Hall', now merely a shell of its original form, is the oldest surviving structure at the palace, and may well date to the time of these two documents. The 13th-century hall was a two-storey free-standing building originally accessed at first floor level. Today, three of its four walls still stand, but they are largely engulfed by later construction. The undercroft probably supported a timber ceiling, but now only a string of corbels remains to show its position.

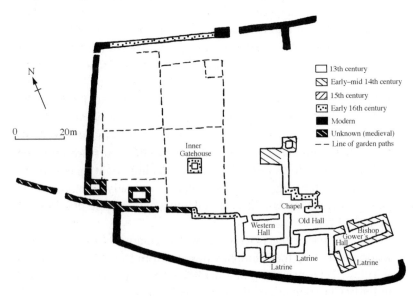

Plan of Lamphey Palace

In essence, the palace was divided into two areas, a large outer ward and a compact inner ward, entirely enclosed by a stone wall which formed a large rectangle and was surrounded by feudal lands also belonging to the bishops. According to the *Black Book of St Davids*, written in 1326, outside the palace walls the bishops maintained a deer park, dovecote, four fishponds and orchards, and raised crops and livestock.

Access to the palace itself was via a simple outer gatehouse on the north-western corner of the site, through which modern visitors must also pass in order to reach the present entrance into the property. Now almost completely ruined, the outer gateway consists of walling into which pigeon holes were added to provide houses for the winter meat supply. They also had two watermills and a windmill and gathered peat for fuel. Inside the precinct walls stood an oxhouse, brewhouse, bakehouse and the inner gatehouse, of which only the latter survives. By all standards, 14th-century Lamphey was a very successful manorial centre.

Almost centrally situated within the palace stands the remains of the inner gatehouse, which is now free-standing but would probably have been flanked by sections of the stone walling that enclosed the inner courtyard. The two-storey building is topped with a battlemented parapet, and a simple archway

The inner gatehouse

115

afforded passage to and from the inner ward. Inside, a mural staircase allowed access to the upper storey; originally access was at first floor level. The basement level is notable for its cobbled floor.

As they did in the Middle Ages, the old hall and the later replacements continue to dominate the inner ward, which had its own separate gatehouse and walls to demarcate it from the rest of the palace. Inside the inner ward the bishop lived, entertained guests and probably performed any administrative duties required of him during his stay, including collecting rents from tenants who farmed the surrounding estates.

When Bishop Richard Carew built the so-called 'Western Hall' (appropriately built immediately to the west of the old hall) later in the 13th century, he apparently transformed the old hall into a kitchen block, with buttery and pantry, which serviced the newer great hall. The largest of the palace's buildings, the battlemented hall measures 17 metres by 7.5 metres. It was once elaborately decorated, but now the surviving masonry only includes remnants of its finery—an ornately carved archway which allowed access at first floor level, lancet-headed windows, an interesting chimney stack and ornate fireplace, and fascinating traces of medieval wall paintings. The ground level still features four doorways that lead into the vaulted undercroft which was lit by five small windows (three of which are now blocked). A spiral staircase afforded access to the first floor at the south-eastern corner of the hall. In the early 16th century, one of the bishops, possibly Bishop Sherborne, added trefoil windows and a small, central chamber to the first floor chamber, a latrine turret and an upper storey, which may have held several small rooms, possibly for residential use.

Shortly after the *Black Book of St Davids* was completed, Lamphey Palace moved into a new, arguably more glorious, building era. Probably instigated by Bishop Henry de Gower (1328-47), whose accomplishments at St Davids Bishops Palace are discussed elsewhere in this book, construction of a third hall occurred at the south-eastern corner of the complex. The new building was slightly offset from the line of the older buildings but placed alongside the remains of the old hall. Now known as Henry de Gower's Hall, the ornate hall is highlighted by an elaborate arcaded parapet, a feature often associated with Bishop Gower. The parapet served both as a vessel for draining away rainwater and also as an elevated walkway which offered panoramic views of the lush countryside.

Bishop Gower's Hall

Possibly used for ceremonial or administrative purposes rather than for accommodation, Henry de Gower's first floor hall was a single, large chamber accessed from the inner ward via a series of stone stairs, originally protected by a wooden roof, forming something akin to a forebuilding. The hall measured 21 metres by 5.5 metres, was lit by six two-trefoiled windows fitted with stone seats, and had a small fireplace. A well preserved, barrel-vaulted undercroft, originally carried on 11 arches and lit with six trefoil-headed windows, spans the entire ground floor level. The undercroft was probably used for storage or, perhaps, as servants' quarters. As with the other two halls, a large latrine turret was added to the south-western corner of Gower's Hall, but was not an original feature of the building.

When Edward Vaughan became Bishop of St Davids in 1509, he remade the western hall into the showcase of the palace and essentially abandoned Bishop Gower's hall. Among the changes contributed by Bishop Vaughan were the addition of a third storey and new windows to the western hall, a huge corn barn which extended almost the entire length of the northern perimeter wall, and the attractive chapel. Standing immediately north of the old hall in what would have been the inner ward, the two-storey chapel is now a shell of its original self, but enough of its architectural finery remains to give an clear impression of its 16th-century appearance. The chapel itself would have filled the first floor; two smaller rooms with mullioned windows occupied the basement level. The building has been greatly altered, and the lower level is now dominated by an enormous archway, situated underneath the elaborate Perpendicular-style traceried east window, which was constructed during the 18th century when the former bishop's palace was used as a farm.

The only other structure of note inside Lamphey Palace is the ruined building standing just north of the chapel, fancifully called 'the Red Chamber'. Probably dating to Henry de Gower's tenure as Bishop of St Davids, the curious structure probably provided additional accommodation. Its main features include a set of three arches, which supported the upper floor, a latrine and a stone staircase on the north-western side, which gave access to the first storey.

The last bishop to occupy Lamphey Palace was Bishop William Barlow (1536-48). Although he garnered royal favour for a time, in 1546 Barlow was apparently required to relinquish control of the palace and manor of Lamphey to his king, Henry VIII, in exchange for the smaller rectory at Carew (see separate entry). Two years later, the manor passed to Richard Devereux and his family, who, as the Earls of Essex, were destined to play a key role in the reign of Queen Elizabeth I. Devereux heirs occupied the palace throughout the 16th century, and Robert Devereux, 2nd Earl of Essex and one of the queen's favourites, lived at Lamphey, albeit for a brief three years from 1581 to 1584. Upon Robert's execution in 1601, ownership of the manor and palace at Lamphey reverted to the Crown, but in 1604 his son, the 3rd Earl of Essex, acquired his rightful inheritance. In the meantime, the palace had been granted to Rhys Philip Scarfe, and afterwards a series of tenants leased the site from Devereux.

During the English Civil War, Lamphey Palace was garrisoned for the Parliamentary cause. In 1683, Sir Hugh Owen of Orielton (south-west of Pembroke) purchased the palace and surrounding land, and swiftly transformed the site into a farmyard. The Owens sold the property to Charles Delamotte Mathias of Llangwarren (also in Pembrokeshire), who built Lamphey Court (now a hotel) and created a walled garden in part of the palace precincts. In 1925, the Mathias heirs placed the palace in the care of the State. During the Second World War, the medieval site housed army and airforce service personnel.

Letterston / Parc Moat

Vanished motte
Location: (SM 938 295)

Probably named for the Flemish settler, Letard (or Lettard) Littleking, several books have documented the existence of a motte castle at Letterston (also known as Littardiston, and, in Welsh, as Trelettert). The Royal Commission records the presence of a medieval settlement at this grid reference, and, in 1925, described the motte as being 91 metres across. Apparently, in the 1960s, the motte measured 18 metres across, rose 1.8 metres, and was encircled with a weak ditch. Parc Moat is identified in CARN, the site database of the RCAHMW as a round barrow or a motte. In any case, the mound no longer survives. When the author attempted to locate the motte, local residents claimed to have never heard of a castle in the village. A go-kart track constructed on the southern side of the main village street probably levelled whatever remains did exist of the castle/round barrow in the late 1990s.

Llanfrynach

Motte / ringwork
Location: $2^{1}/_{2}$ miles south-east of Crymych (SN 219 312)
Access: Visible from road by church

Located just north-west of the village church on the side of the road and partly incorporated into private gardens, the small earthwork castle at Llanfrynach has been identified as a ring-motte and also as a motte and bailey. The sizeable mound stands about 6 metres high and reaches 18 metres across. The summit dips in the centre, which lends credence to its characterisation as a ring-motte.

Llangwathen

Motte
Location: 1 mile east of Narberth (SN 134 153)
Access: Private, no access

Only discovered in the 1980s, the reportedly poorly preserved motte at Llangwathen (and not marked on current OS maps) overlooks the Afon Marlais about a mile east of Narberth. Even though the site is difficult to locate, records indicate that the motte stands 3 metres high and has a summit measuring 20 metres across. The author has not visited this site.

Llawhaden

Ringwork / stone bishop's castle
Location: 8 miles east of Haverfordwest (SN 073 174)
Access: In care of Cadw and open to the public

To reach the impressive bishop's castle, take the turn off on the A40 about eight miles east of Haverfordwest signposted to Llawhaden. In the village, park in the small car park at the start of the no through road that leads to the castle. Presently maintained by Cadw, the site is normally open any reasonable time for a small fee.

Whereas their other residences in Pembrokeshire are more appropriately classified as palaces or stately homes by the end of the 14th century, the residence of the Bishops of St Davids at Llawhaden possessed all the essential features one normally associates with a medieval castle: its twin-towered gatehouse overlooked a deep ditch, not only augmenting the castle's defensive strength, but also providing quarters for the garrison, while the lanky great hall, flanked on the east by private apartments and on the west by the kitchen and a bakehouse, filled the opposite side of the inner bailey. Nearby, the well dropped some 30 metres into the ground. A second range of residential chambers—added during the final building phase—occupied the southeastern side of the castle, the northern end of which held the chapel and the unusual porch.

More than likely, in about 1115, shortly after Queen Matilda replaced Sulien, the last Welsh bishop of St Davids with Bernard, the first Norman bishop for the region, he began the first castle, a ringwork, at Llawhaden. Built on lands owned by the Bishops of St Davids in the early 12th century, the formidable ringwork castle with a steep-sided circular embankment and deep ditch—still seen today—dominated the site for about 20 years before the clerics decided to strengthen it in stone. When Gerald of Wales visited Llawhaden in 1175 to meet with his uncle, Bishop David FitzGerald, the earthwork castle was still defended by a timber palisade and drawbridge. However, shortly after the Welsh, led by the Lord Rhys, assaulted the site in 1192, Rhys' son, Hywel, destroyed the timber defences to prevent the castle from posing any future threat to the Welsh, and then promptly abandoned the site.

In the early 13th century, the Bishops of St Davids regained control of the castle site and began a major rebuilding programme at Llawhaden. This phase involved the construction of a stone curtain wall and at least two substantial round mural towers, of which only the foundations survive on the western side of the castle. Measuring some 8 metres across, the larger tower may have served as the keep. The smaller semicircular tower had a diameter of 5.5 metres. At one time, the two towers were linked by a faceted curtain wall, a configuration often used when fortifying ringworks with masonry defences (other examples include Coity and Newcastle Bridgend, in Glamorgan). Portions of this wall were

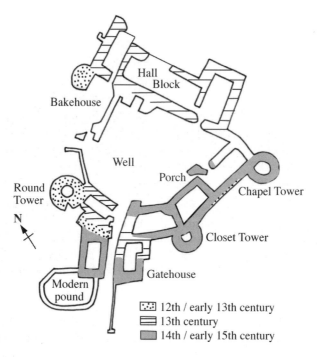

Bakehouse

Hall
Block

Well

Round
Tower

Porch

Chapel Tower

N

Closet Tower

Modern
pound

Gatehouse

▦ 12th / early 13th century
▤ 13th century
▨ 14th / early 15th century

Plan of Llawhaden Castle

later incorporated into the western tower of the gatehouse and also into the south-eastern range.

In the late 13th century, Thomas Bek, who served as Bishop of St Davids from 1280 to 1293, began the castle's transformation into a comfortable, yet fortified, residence. His chief contribution was the two storey great hall. Together with the kitchen and solar, which extended from either side of the upper level, the great hall measured 24 metres by 7 metres. Underneath, the bishops used the vaulted undercroft to store food and other supplies. For a time, the great hall was accessed by a set of timber steps from the inner ward, but this was eventually replaced by a stone stairway and forebuilding, remnants of which survive. The forebuilding itself was later largely removed to make way for a bakehouse, which is now little more than foundations. Bishop Bek also established the market town at Llawhaden and a hospice to care for the poor, elderly and infirm on the adjoining lands. The hospice apparently functioned as a leper house; only the ruined chapel survives to any extent.

The hall block

Bishop David Martyn (1293–1328) continued Bek's rebuilding programme, probably completing the accommodation for the lords of the castle while also adding living quarters for a small garrison to the western side of the main gate.

Gatehouse (left), Closet Tower and curtain wall

The south range and the porch

Later in the 14th century, Bishop Adam de Houghton (1362–89) hired master mason John Fawle to begin the south-eastern range of buildings along the line of the 13th-century masonry curtain wall. This sector of structures included two apartments, which stood over an undercroft. The chambers were fitted with fireplaces, lit with crossloops and separated by an octagonal latrine tower, the shaft of which runs down the wall between the two apartments. These rooms presumably accommodated guests of some standing or the bishop's retinue.

Rising from the ditch outside its walls, the castle chapel occupied the eastern end of this range. Though now a shell like the neighbouring structures, the exterior walls retain their putlog holes. Varying types of stone reflect different building phases. Of particular note, a five-storey porch fronted the chapel, providing access from the inner ward and outstanding views of the surrounding countryside. The series of small chambers on the upper floors of the porch were linked by a spiral staircase and may have housed the bishop's exchequer. A finely carved doorway lintel is adorned with stone heads depicting a crowned male and a female wearing what appears to be a wimple; some scholars speculate that the figures may represent the king and queen of England. The polygonal tower at the chapel's eastern corner contained another latrine and also held the castle's dungeon, just like any secular castle.

Besides the south-eastern range, Bishop Houghton's most impressive legacy is the great gatehouse, the castle's most imposing feature (see photograph at the start of this entry). Although the interior is almost completely decayed, the façade remains intact enough for the visitor to imagine its medieval appearance. The two semi-circular towers are supported by spurred buttresses which reach into the ditch, and arrowslits still open from the guardrooms that once stood alongside the gateway. Murder holes and a portcullis slot are visible in the ceiling above the gate passage, which was reached by a movable drawbridge, a pivot stone for which still survives. The main entrance rises to the level of the second storey, and traces of the early 13th-century curtain wall still reach into the western tower at the point where the rising walkway alters its angle. Exterior walls are highlighted at this level by a banding effect created with purple Caerbwdy sandstone from St Davids. The better preserved eastern tower retains interior walls, floors, fireplaces and window seats. These rooms accommodated the castle constable and his household, or other members of the garrison. With the completion of the gatehouse and the south-eastern range, the castle acquired its final form.

Late in the 15th century, Llawhaden Castle began serving as a prison for the Bishops of St Davids who held trials inside its walls. Among the prisoners in the early 16th century was a woman with an unsavoury reputation and known variously as Tanglwys or Tanglos. A friend, Thomas Wyriott of Orielton, assaulted the castle in 1503 hoping to free her.

Sporadically maintained during the 16th century, Bishop William Barlow stripped the castle of its lead during the dissolution of the monasteries. In 1616, Bishop Richard Milbourne was permitted to demolish the site but, fortunately, did not complete the task. In 1931, the Bishops of St Davids placed Llawhaden Castle in the care of the State.

Llawhaden Castle is unique not only because its large ringwork was later transformed into an impressive stone stronghold, but also because the fortified structure was also the only bishop's castle in Pembrokeshire.

Lydstep

Fortified dwelling
Location: On the A4139 between Pembroke and Tenby
(SS 086 984)
Access: Exterior visible from road

Situated on the northern side of the A4139 as it curves through the village, the stout remains of a rectangular building of medieval date protrude upward between the trees and a well-manicured private dwelling. Characterised in CARN, the site database of the RCAHMW, as a house or dwelling, the ruined building has long been known as Lydstep Palace, or Lydstep Old Palace, and is designated as such by Cadw. However, there is nothing substantial in the historical record to verify this notion, and at best, the site should be classified as a fortified dwelling or first floor hall, as Neil Ludlow at Cambria Archaeology has stated in site reports published after excavations in 1996 and 2002. First floor halls were fairly common in southern Pembrokeshire during the late Middle Ages.

More than likely, the characterisation of this structure as a 'palace' derives from local tradition in a region where several true bishop's palaces existed, rather than from any historical connection with the Bishops of St Davids. Stories have claimed that, in the 14th century, Bishop Henry Gower constructed Lydstep Palace as a hunting lodge, but nothing in the historical record indicates that the bishops owned any property nor had any jurisdiction in this part of Pembrokeshire. Indeed, the site's identification as a palace first occurs in early 19th-century documents.

Probably best classified as a 'vill' or manorial settlement, Lydstep belonged to the barony of Manorbier established in the 12th century by Odo de Barri and centred at Manorbier Castle (see separate entry). According to Ludlow (2002), the primary function of the building during the medieval period would have been residential; however, the layout of the first floor hall and the presence of several external stairways may suggest that the building was used—at least for a time—for some purpose other than as a home. Perhaps the building replaced an earlier structure or was constructed to provide a place to house the courts already being held on adjoining property (labelled on an 18th-century estate map as 'Longstone Park') and mentioned in 17th-century documents as the 'court of Langstone'. Speculation exists that the courts were originally held in the open air, and that the 'palace' was purpose-built as a replacement. The hall's administrative function probably ceased in the 17th century, as the power of the manorial court declined. The building would more than likely have been used afterwards as a dwelling of lesser importance, with extra structures added to both ends.

Construction occurred in eight separate phases, which began no later than the 14th century. The structure was actually occupied well into the 20th century, but by that time it had extensively decayed. Measuring 18.1 by 6.3 metres, the building was constructed primarily of local carboniferous limestone. The ground floor probably initially contained two vaulted chambers but, later, the southernmost of the two rooms was divided again, creating three chambers in total. The basement level was overlain by a large hall that originally filled the entire level but was eventually separated into three unvaulted rooms with the aid of an open arch and timber screens, as the discovery of a springer on the internal western wall suggests. There was no direct access between the two storeys. With walls averaging about 0.6 metres in thickness, the first floor had thinner walls than the lower level, where the walls measured 1.3 metres on the west and about 1.0 metres on the remaining sides. More than likely, the first floor always supported a timber gabled roof rather than more substantial masonry battlements. Surviving features include a splayed light, corbelling, remnants of a fireplace on the south wall, and blocked doorways, probably added during one of the later building periods.

Probably built during the second construction phase (15th century), a two-storey rectangular latrine tower projects outward from the north-western side of the building; it possibly replaced one built in the previous century. In the late 19th or early 20th century, a bread oven was installed in place of the latrine which had previously been altered for use as a chimney flue.

By the 18th century, the Meyrick family of Norchard owned the building together with lands east of the parish boundary. They continued to use the building as accommodation; in 1841, Thomas Lewis, their tenant, lived in the 'cottage'. Nonetheless, its condition deteriorated, and the entire building was described at this time as 'mean tenements'. Occupied until after the Second World War, only minor alterations were made, which included roof slates, pink plasterwork and a timber A-frame roof.

In 1995, the South Pembrokeshire District Council purchased Lydstep Palace with the intention of consolidating the ruin and possibly preparing it for future use. The archaeological excavations were part of an ongoing programme of clearance and consolidation initiated and largely funded by Pembrokeshire County Council.

Maenclochog

?Vanished motte
Location: (SN 083 272)

The Royal Commission records the existence of a possible motte castle called Manor Pound or Y Gaer at Maenclochog. The author attempted to locate the site, but could not find any structural remains. The historical record indicates that Llywelyn ab Iorwerth or Rhys Ieuanc seized the motte in 1215, and that his grandson, Llywelyn ap Gruffydd, destroyed the castle in 1257. The site is indicated on some OS maps as being located behind the village chapel on the southern side of the junction with the B4313 and the village centre.

Manorbier

Enclosure Castle
Location: On the coast between Pembroke and Tenby (SS 064 978)
Access: Privately owned, open at certain times of the year

To reach Manorbier and its castle, take the B4585 leading southward from the A4139 Pembroke / Tenby road signposted for the village.

It's not surprising to learn that Gerald of Wales (Giraldus Cambrensis), with admitted bias, proclaimed Manorbier to be 'the pleasantest spot in Wales'. After all, the renown priest, traveller, chronicler, and 'renaissance' man was born in the picturesque castle, which still offers panoramic vistas of the white beaches and blue waters of Manorbier Bay. Perched at the edge of a westward facing ridge adjacent to the compact village of the same name, the site combines all the aesthetic qualities of a fine fortified manor with its original feudal estate, remnants of which survive at the base of the castle.

The origins of the name, Manorbier, are somewhat unclear. The earliest known variant is *Mainaur Pir*, which may derive from the Welsh, *Maenor Pyr*, *Maenor Pir* or *Maenor Pirr*. This probably refers to the Manor of Pyr, and has direct associations with Caldey Island (Ynys Pyr), just a few miles offshore. The island has long been home to a monastic community. In the 6th century, the abbot

132

Gerald of Wales' view to the sea, with the eastern range to the left and hall-keep to the rear

of the monastery was named Pyr (or Pir). Unfortunately his main claim to fame was for his unusual death in the abbey fishpond, which allegedly occurred after a night of drinking wine.

Even though the region has been inhabited since prehistoric times, it was not until the late 11th century that a fortification was begun at Manorbier. The manor was the property of the de Barri family who had earlier established themselves at Barry, near Cardiff in Glamorgan. Odo de Barri received the lordship of Manorbier, an area that included the three manorial estates of Manorbier, Penally and Begelly, as a reward for service during the Norman conquest of Wales (he might have been part of the incursion led by Arnulf de Montgomery; Manorbier also included Jameston and Manorbier Newton.) In return, the de Barris owed the monarchy five knights' fees.

In about 1093, Odo de Barri began the first castle at Manorbier. Virtually nothing remains of this site; only the rock-cut ditch fronting the main gatehouse may date to the late 11th century. Odo's castle may have contained a timber hall, which his son, William, (or William's heir, Philip) probably replaced in stone in

133

the 12th century. More than likely, the castle in which Gerald of Wales was born in about 1146 was essentially still an earth and timber stronghold that contained a few masonry structures. Gerald of Wales was the fourth son of William de Barri and his wife, Angharad, who was the daughter of the Norman Gerald de Windsor and his Welsh wife, Nest. Nest was the daughter of Rhys ap Tewdwr, prince of Deheubarth, and played a scandalous role in the politics of the times not only in Wales but also with the English monarchy (see entries for Carew and Cilgerran castles).

The main approach to the castle requires visitors to trudge uphill from the car park which now fills the lower end of the valley that cuts between the castle and the medieval church. Situated on the opposite hilltop, the Church of St James the Greater, Apostle and Martyr, is clearly visible from the castle grounds. Apparently the young Gerald de Barri, already contemplating the priesthood, fled to its protection when the Welsh raided nearby Tenby in 1153. Although undergoing restoration, the church remains accessible to the public, and still holds regular services.

Manorbier Castle's attractive battlemented gatehouse (see photograph at the start of this entry) offers access to all comers, as it did in the Middle Ages. While not the oldest structure at the site, the gateway is one of its finest features. Dating to the late 13th century, the rectangular building replaced the simple archway that originally served as the main entrance. In excellent condition, the gatehouse rises two storeys over the vaulted passage. Originally fronted by a timber drawbridge which spanned the ditch, only its fittings survive. Two small chambers filled the upper levels, access to which is presently barred. One of the rooms would have housed the castle's constable and the mechanism for raising the portcullis at the front of the passageway, which was defended by two portcullises, the grooves for which survive, and also a set of heavy timber doors.

Immediately to the north of the gatehouse stands the so-called 'Old Tower', which was built in the late 12th century probably during the castle's initial conversion from timber to stone. Even though much of this structure no longer survives, enough remains to give visitors an impression of its fairly crude construction, which

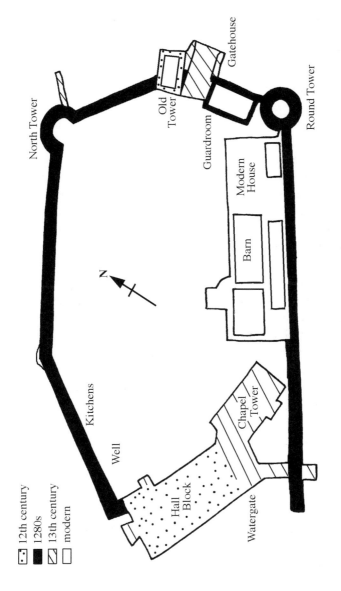

N

12th century
1280s
13th century
modern

North Tower

Old Tower

Gatehouse

Guardroom

Round Tower

Modern House

Barn

Kitchens

Well

Chapel Tower

Hall Block

Watergate

Plan of Manorbier Castle

included doorways on the ground and first floors. The rectangular tower measured 7.5 by 6.3 metres, and had walls about 1 metre thick. During the 13th century, the old tower was modified to accommodate the new gatehouse and received a higher roofline to match the height of the neighbouring building. Unfortunately, its upper levels have long since collapsed.

In the mid-13th century, before constructing the new gatehouse, the de Barris enclosed the site with stone walls, which probably traced the plan of the original earthwork castle. Still in good condition, the walls rose some 3 to 4 metres to wall-walk level, and enclosed an area of about 67 by 44 metres.

To the south side of the gatehouse stands the impressive four-storey high Round Tower, which is partly open to the public and provides access to wall-walk level, from which it once opened into the upper level of the gateway. Between the circular tower and the gatehouse, the former guardroom has been converted into the castle shop.

A second round-fronted tower (the so-called North Tower) guarded the north-western side of the gatehouse. Less substantial than the Round Tower, the rear wall of the three-storey tower was probably either built of timber or only covered the uppermost level. A small doorway at basement level offers access to a latrine and to one of the castle's exhibition rooms.

The curtain wall continues from the North Tower along the western side of the castle to the remnants of the kitchen block and onward to the hall-block. About midway along this side of the castle, a small tower once stood at the point where the two lengths of wall converge. It probably served not just as a latrine tower but also as an observation post from which arrows could be fired when necessary. Little remains of the kitchen range, with the noteworthy exception of the well—in the inner bailey—and a couple of ovens, which were later additions. Remnants of three large windows and a large Flemish chimney, the date of which is uncertain, line the wall at this point. The oven may have been used to forge iron in the 16th or 17th centuries.

Said to be the oldest stone building surviving at any castle in west Wales, the three-storey hall-keep, located immediately across the inner bailey from the main gatehouse, measures some 20 by 10

The remains of the kitchen block

metres. As the castle's primary residential building, the structure contained all the chambers expected of a typical keep, but is unusual in that it is much longer than it is tall. The once ornate great hall centred the first floor of the building, and was accessed from the inner bailey via an impressive stone porchway, added at a later date, which is now extensively ruined. A huge fireplace dominated the wall near the doorway leading into the exquisitely decorated great hall. A large window overlooked the inner ward alongside to the fireplace. Little of substance survives of the domestic chambers that once filled the second storey over the great hall. Underneath, the three barrel-vaulted, windowless chambers probably provided ground level storage space. The buttery and pantry filled the western end of the hall-keep to service the lord and his guests dining in the adjoining chamber. A small chamber fitted with a fireplace and latrine that emptied outside the castle wall occupied the area above.

Constructed at an angle to the easternmost side of the hall, the ornate chapel building and solar were added during the late 13th century. Erected either by David de Barri I (d.1262), who added the curtain wall, or by his son, David de Barri II, who served as Lord Justiciar of Ireland in the 1260s, the complex of buildings also included a latrine tower and a watergate or postern tower. While complete access is restricted, the towers may be examined from positions both inside and outside the castle.

South-east corner of the curtain wall with watergate tower

An enormous barn once lined the eastern side of the castle. Although altered into a residence, much of its original fabric is still identifiable. Projecting into the inner ward from the north-western end of the barn, the large hearth and oven may have served the same function as their counterparts on the opposite side of the bailey.

At least six David de Barris played a role at Manorbier Castle from the 13th century until the last David died in 1392. According to D.J. Cathcart King and J. Clifford Perks (in a reprint taken from *Archaeologica Cambrensis*, 1951), the calendar of patent rolls indicates that, sometime during the mid-14th century, de Barri had turned over the castle to William de Windsor, who had intended Manorbier to ultimately pass to his nephew, John. In the meantime, William parcelled out the manor to Sir William de Beauchamp, with the stipulation that de Windsor would remain tenant for life and reap the financial benefits due to him. However, upon William de Windsor's death, his widow, Alice Perrers, passed ownership of Manorbier Castle to John, Duke of Exeter, rather than to William de Windsor's rightful heir, John de Windsor.

After Henry IV ordered Exeter's execution in 1399, the duke's widow, Elizabeth, and her new husband, Sir John Cornwall, acquired Manorbier Castle. John de Windsor promptly challenged them for possession of his inheritance. The king was forced to intervene in the conflict and formally granted a life-tenancy to Elizabeth and her husband, whom he acknowledged as the Earl of Huntingdon. Upon Elizabeth's death, ownership of the castle passed to her son, Sir John Holand, by her second husband. The de Barris never again had possession of Manorbier Castle.

In the late 15th century, Manorbier Castle became a Crown property, but continued to be let to various tenants, including Edward IV's sister, Anne, Duchess of Exeter, and Lady Margaret Beaufort, Countess of Richmond and Henry VII's mother, who died in 1509 having never actually lived at the castle. Then, Margaret's grandson, Henry VIII, granted the manors of Manorbier and Penally to his illegitimate son, Henry FitzRoy, Duke of Richmond and Somerset. FitzRoy carried on the practice of leasing out the property. Upon his son's untimely death, the king granted the castle to one of his pages, Hugh Jones, as a reward for his loyalty to the young FitzRoy. By this time (1528), the castle had already begun to decay, yet it remained valuable enough in 1603 for Thomas Bowen of Trefloyne, then steward of the manor, to purchase the site from Queen Elizabeth I. The Bowens then ran into serious financial difficulties and in 1670 they sold Manorbier Castle to Sir Erasmus Philipps of Picton Castle for £6,000.

The outer bailey played a role during the 1640s, when possession of the castle alternated between Royalist supporters of King Charles I and Parliamentarian troops under the command of Rowland Laugharne, who seized the castle in 1645. Manorbier Castle was then strengthened in an effort to withstand an assault. New construction included the 'braye', an outer line of defences erected beyond the masonry walls of the castle, the centre of which was revetted with masonry (a 'redan'). Modern visitors pass through this feature to enter the castle.

After the English Civil War, the site was used as a farm; the barn in the outer ward may date to that time. Down the hill behind the castle, the well-preserved dovecote and noteworthy remains of the castle fishpond and mill offer insight into the daily operations of the manorial site. The nearby land probably held the deer park and orchards.

In 1880, the Philipps family leased Manorbier Castle to J.R. Cobb, the avid antiquarian who played a key role in the restoration of many castles, including nearby Pembroke Castle (see separate entry). Inside Manorbier's inner bailey, Cobb used part of the barn to build himself a house, portions of which are now available for lease as self-catering accommodation. He also restored the floors and roofs of the North and Round Towers and the gatehouse, added new windows, and repaired some of the masonry.

The Philipps family continues to own the castle at Manorbier, but actually resides at Picton Castle (see separate entry). Until her death in 1999, Sheila Philipps, Lady Dunsany, took a special interest in Manorbier Castle, ensuring its consolidation and access by the public. When she died, the castle passed to Lady Dunsany's daughters.

Minwear

Possible ringwork
Location: 3 miles west of Narberth (SN 062 135)
Access: On private land

Identified on Ordnance Survey Pathfinder maps as a 'homestead' and Explorer maps as 'enclosure', the embanked oval enclosure near Minwear is classified in CARN, the site database of the RCAHMW, as a ringwork. CARN also lists this site as an Iron Age fort. The 1.8 metre high embankment encloses a bailey measuring about 28 metres across. Traces of a possible ditch are visible.

Narberth

Enclosure Castle
Location: Narberth (SO 109 144)
Access: Should be open to the public from April 2005

In recent years, Narberth Castle has been receiving something of a facelift. Archaeologists have conducted new excavations and plans for the site include consolidation so that the public may gain safe access. Coincidental with the castle's new look, theories surrounding its earliest history have also been revised.

Historians have long associated the earthwork castle at Templeton (see separate entry) with a castle mentioned in the *Brut y Tywysogion* and in the *Mabinogion* as 'the castle in Arberth'. Research conducted by Neil Ludlow of Cambria Archaeology has, however, not only revealed the likelihood that the first castle at Narberth was probably established between 1093 and 1110, but that the historical record makes no mention of a castle being relocated from Templeton to Narberth. Furthermore, speculation that the first builder of the castle may have been Sir Andrew Perrot or his ancestor, Sir Stephen Perrot, has been debunked by Roger Turvey. An expert on the history of the Perrot family in Pembrokeshire, he even questions whether either of these men ever actually existed. That one of them built a castle at Narberth in the 11th or 13th centuries, therefore, seems less than plausible. However, if the earliest castle was a motte and bailey, nothing of it remains at Narberth today.

Nonetheless, the historical record does mention a castle at Narberth (Castell yn Arberth) as early as 1116, when it was assaulted and burned by the Welsh, probably under the leadership of Gruffydd ap Rhys, son of Rhys ap Tewdwr, Prince of Deheubarth, who had been killed in 1093. When Gruffydd was forced into exile shortly thereafter, ownership of the castle reverted to the Normans. Some 20 years later, his nephew, Henry FitzRoy (Henry I's illegitimate son by Nest, daughter of Rhys ap Tewdwr), acquired possession of the commote of Narberth (Cwmwd Arberth) and, along with it, control of the castle. Taking the title Lord of Narberth, FitzRoy held the castle and surrounding area until his death in 1157. The history of the castle immediately following his death is unclear; however, in 1159, the Welsh may have again attacked Narberth and burned the castle, although it continued to remain in Anglo-Norman hands until well into the following century.

In 1215 and again in 1220, Llywelyn ab Iorwerth and comrades made several forays into southern Wales, burning but not taking Narberth Castle. Shortly thereafter William Marshal II, Earl of Pembroke, acquired ownership of the castle and lordship of Narberth which remained under the control of the Marshals until 1245, when the last male heir to the earldom died. Two years later, the vast Marshal estates were divided between the three heiresses of William Marshal I (who had died in 1219), and Narberth passed by right of marriage to Roger Mortimer, the husband of Maud de Braose, Eva Marshal's daughter.

More than likely, most of what survives of Narberth Castle dates to the Mortimer tenure at the site, when its owners finally rebuilt the structure in stone after it had suffered yet another onslaught by the Welsh in 1257, this time led by Llywelyn ap Gruffydd. Essentially rectangular in shape, Narberth Castle still dominates a steep-sided spur on the southern side of the town, around which the A478 passes near the base and swings uphill close to the main entrance. The view of the surrounding countryside was extensive, and visitors arriving at the castle from the south would have identified its grey masonry form from quite some distance away. Measuring about 50 by 25 metres, the castle consisted of four massive corner towers, had two semicircular towers jutting out about midway along the western and eastern curtain wall, and was fronted on the northern side by a twin-towered gatehouse, now completely destroyed. The north-western tower is the most extensively decayed of the four main towers, but retains traces of a latrine shaft. It was probably very similar in design to the towers on the southern side of the castle.

Originally linked by a length of curtain wall, the two southern towers now stand as individual structures, each still connected to lengths of north-south running wall which now abruptly terminates where smaller D-shaped towers once guarded the wall about midway between the entrance and southern range on both sides of the inner ward. The south-eastern tower is the more ruined of the two. Only the south-facing side stands to its original three storeys, about 11 metres in height. The tower's basal diameter measured about 5 metres and walls stretched about 2.5 metres in thickness. The battlements no longer survive. Remnants of a spiral staircase and two windows are evident, and what appears to be a piscina survives on the first floor, indicating the room's use as a chapel. The ground floor once served as a bakehouse, while upper storeys were probably used as private accommodation.

Immediately north of the south-eastern tower stand the curious remains of a two-storey, flat-topped structure with a notable barrel-vaulted, cobble-floored basement. Measuring 12 by 8 metres, the so-called 'vaulted building' had two entrances, one of which linked to the south-eastern tower. It was probably used as a pantry and perhaps also as a kitchen/brewhouse, as the stone-lined drain may indicate. A single chamber occupied the entire first floor, and may have served as the solar or lord's private apartment.

Fragments of the great hall with the east range beyond

The great hall once filled the entire upper level of the structure located between the two southern towers, but is now almost completely destroyed. This 10-metre high building once measured approximately 20 by 8 metres; only its northern wall survives to any significant degree. The basement level retains three square window embrasures and a doorway at the western end, while the first floor features remnants of three larger windows with seats. A survey undertaken in 1539 indicates that the ground floor held the kitchen; however, little remains to verify that characterisation.

The best-preserved of the castle's structures is the three-storey south-western tower (see photograph at the start of this entry), which had dimensions comparable to its twin to the east. Each of the levels had windows, one of which retains its seat and traces of a lancet-head. A spiral staircase at the south-western corner offered access between the storeys. The 16th-century survey recorded the presence of a larderhouse on the ground level of this tower and two (apparently residential) chambers on the upper storeys.

Rising four storeys, Narberth Castle's north-eastern tower probably functioned as the keep. Even though the massive round tower is extensively ruined, enough survives on its south-eastern side to give a fair indication of its original appearance. With a diameter of about 15 metres and walls measuring 3 metres thick at their base, the keep was accessed via a forebuilding, the remains of which are visible on the southern side and still stand in part to first floor level, where the entrance was located. Several garderobes provided sanitary facilities on each level of the keep and also in the forebuilding. The garderobe shafts in the keep dumped into a square chamber (a cess pit?) at the

Remains of the great keep

base of the tower. Ludlow speculates that the keep contained three upper level chambers and a dungeon at ground level, much of which is hidden underneath debris and loose masonry.

The keep-tower stood alongside an outer ward, the remains of which have long since become overgrown and may possibly have been built over with houses on the eastern side. At least one historian claims that the flat-topped portion on the east is remarkably reminiscent of a motte, and may mark the location of the original earth and timber castle at Narberth, but archaeological evidence presently does not support this notion. In 2001–2, archaeologists unearthed at least 20 east/west aligned burials in the outer ward area. Pottery and a radiocarbon date from the graves indicate that the burials took place in the late 12th or 13th centuries. This cemetery may mark the original location of Narberth's parish church, which is now situated some 180 metres to the west.

Shortly after Roger Mortimer's death in 1282, his widow, Maud, passed Narberth Castle and lordship to their son, another Roger Mortimer, of Chirk. In 1299, while Mortimer was serving his king in France, the Welsh again burned but did not take the castle. Over

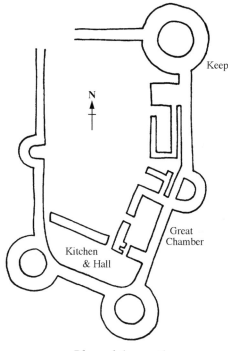

N

Keep

Great
Chamber

Kitchen
& Hall

Plan of the castle

the next decades the most notorious Roger Mortimer of them all tricked his relatives, the Mortimers of Chirk, out of their inheritance. But the Mortimer estates reverted to the Crown when this Roger Mortimer conspired with his paramour, Queen Isabella, to overthrow King Edward II in 1321, was caught and imprisoned in the Tower of London. For a time, Rhys ap Gruffydd acted as the castle's constable; but in 1326, he received the manor and castle of Narberth for the remainder of his lifetime. However, Roger Mortimer had escaped to France and returned with Queen Isabella to overthrow Edward II and rule as king in all but name. Narberth Castle was repaired by 1330, when the great hall and 'vaulted building' were probably also added. When Mortimer was executed in 1330, Narberth reverted once again to the king, now Edward III, who placed the castle in the care of Robert de Hasley and then into the hands of Henry de Gower, Bishop of St Davids. Bishop Gower retained control of the lordship until 1354, when the rightful Mortimer heir, yet another Roger, reacquired Narberth. Five years later, Roger turned over the estates and castle to the Bishop of Winchester, but in 1360 Mortimer's widow, Philippa, regained possession.

Ownership of the castle fluctuated between the Mortimers and the monarchy until 1449, when Richard, Duke of York, the Mortimer heir, mortgaged the town, castle and lordship of Narberth to John de la Bere, Bishop of St Davids, and Gruffydd ap Nicholas, Deputy Justiciar for South Wales. Long neglected, the castle had begun to decay by this time. Despite its decrepit condition, it continued to remain of value to its owners, and in 1453, Walter Devereux gained control of the castle and lordship in the name of the Duke of York. Consequently, Narberth Castle became a Yorkist stronghold during the ensuing Wars of the Roses. In 1515, Henry VIII gave control of the castle to Sir Rhys ap Thomas of Carew. For the next century, Narberth Castle continued its role as an administrative centre.

During the early 17th century, Narberth Castle was the focus of a dispute between the Prince of Wales, the future King Charles I, and George Barlow, a local landowner. Barlow was forced to purchase the castle and lordship from the prince, and it passed to Barlow's son, John, in 1628. After the English Civil War, during which Barlow supported the king, Parliament took control of Narberth Castle and the surrounding estates. Once the new king, Charles II, gained the throne, he restored the property to its rightful owners, and the Barlows apparently continued to own the castle until late in the 17th century, when it was abandoned and allowed to become ruinous.

In the 1970s, New Zealander Robert Perrot, not believed to be a relation of the Pembrokeshire Perrots, bought the castle and made a cursory effort to excavate the site. Public access was restricted and the property became overgrown and piled in part with debris from the crumbling castle. In the late 1990s, Pembrokeshire County Council negotiated a 99-year lease of the site with the intention of clearing and consolidating the castle. Work is due to be completed by the end of March 2005 (to coincide with the publication of this book!), when it is intended that the Town Council will take on day to day responsibility and that the castle site will be open to the public.

Nevern / Nanhyfer

Ringwork/ Motte and bailey
Location: (SN 082 401)
Access: Open Access

Not too far off the beaten track just east of Newport, the B4582 guides travellers to medieval Nevern. Long ago, pilgrims passed through the spot *en route* to St David's (three pilgrimages to the city equalled a single journey to Rome). Many probably paused at the Church of St Brynach. Others stopped to pray before a limestone cliffside a bit further on, where the devout carved a cross into the hillface. Modern-day ramblers still walk the ancient footpath, gaze at the Pilgrim's Cross and marvel at the medieval mission fulfilled by so many so long ago.

Many people who journey to Nevern probably never explore the large castle at the top of the hill above St Brynach's. But, it's more than worth the short trek to wander the earthworks and imagine what life may have been like for both the Norman and Welsh leaders who occupied the site during the 12th and 13th centuries. Probably founded in the early 12th century by Robert FitzMartin, Lord of Cemmaes (Cemais), the first castle at Nevern probably served as the administrative centre or caput for the lordship. FitzMartin's ringwork castle consisted of ditched, earthwork embankments forming arcs on all but the eastern side of the promontory overlooking the River Gamman. The banks may have originated as part of an earlier Iron Age promontory fort. Topped with timber palisades, they were well positioned to protect the Norman inhabitants from landward attack. The gorge on the opposite side of the site plunged over 30 metres to the river below, and certainly prevented any kind of access from the east. During the Middle Ages, the river also served as the castle's main water supply.

A gap between the northern and western banks of the ringwork probably allowed routine entry into the castle, but William FitzMartin—or perhaps the Welsh—soon plugged the opening during a second building programme in the late 12th century. Partly disguised beneath bracken and trees, the bulky motte still fills the spot between the two embankments. Stretching about 6.5 metres across the summit, the motte rises some 7 metres above the bailey, but is only 3.5 metres higher than the adjoining earthworks which directly abut the mound. Planted on the castle's highest point, the mound once supported a small masonry tower, probably added shortly after the motte was completed. Discovered in the early 1980s, only traces of this round tower survive. A substantial bank and ditch still run southward from the motte, and a double bank and ditch stretches across the northern side of the site. Also merging with the motte, the outer rampart is revetted in stone. A large opening at the eastern end of the banks allows visitors to gain access to the bailey.

Across the bailey closer to the River Gamman on the eastern side of the castle, a triangle-shaped, artificially sculpted mound supported a square tower, low earthen banks and other stone buildings. Created by carving a deep rock-cut ditch, which dropped to a depth of six metres and measured about seven metres across, the shaley mound and associated inner bailey stretched about 25 metres at its widest point. Probably reached via a wooden bridge, the outer edges of the mound were revetted in stone, as was the hillside that trimmed the southern side of the bailey leading away from the motte.

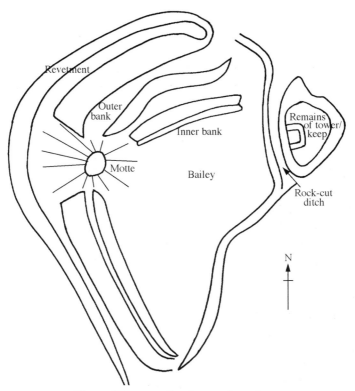

Plan of Nevern Castle earthworks

The western motte
(that to the east is shown at the start of this entry)

Looking south alongside the western embankments
towards the Preselis

Roger Turvey (1989) speculates that the extensive alteration of the original (partial) ringwork into a double-motted stronghold, which included the placement of a motte about midway along one of the ringwork embankments; the excavation of a rock-cut ditch, which created an 'inner castle' topped with a flattened summit; the concomitant construction of several stone structures and towers atop both mounds; and the addition of stone revetments on the northern and eastern flanks of the outer bailey, suggests the presence of a 'new occupier', namely the Welsh, who wrested control of the castle from the Normans in 1191. According to Gerald of Wales, the Lord Rhys of Deheubarth, who had previously assured peace with the Normans by agreeing to the marriage of his daughter, Angharad, to William FitzMartin, stormed and seized Nevern Castle, and then granted its use to his eldest son, Gruffydd. Turvey believes it would have been after this event that the Welsh radically changed the castle to better serve their own needs.

The Lord Rhys probably never imagined that, three years later, two of his other sons, Maelgwyn and Hywel Sais, would imprison him in Castell Nanhyfer. Maelgwyn had already acquired the castle from his elder brother, Gruffydd, and certainly would have yearned for a larger share of his father's fortune and status. Almost immediately, though, Hywel regretted his actions, took Nevern Castle from Maelgwyn and freed his father. Then, in 1195, Hywel dismantled the castle so that the Normans could not retake it. At about the same time, the Lord Rhys captured two of his other rebellious sons, Rhys Gryg and Maredudd, and imprisoned them at Ystrad Meurig Castle (an earthwork castle which still stands in Ceredigion).

In about 1196, William FitzMartin took back control of Nevern Castle and the lordship of Cemmaes, but after investing a small sum to make repairs (about 20 marks, which was loaned to FitzMartin by the Crown), the family then spent little time at the site. Instead, they moved their family seat to nearby Newport where they quickly established another ringwork, and then a new masonry castle (see separate entries).

The Welsh, in the meantime, regained control of Nevern Castle, which they held until the death of Hywel Sais in 1204. Upon his death, the FitzMartins regained control of the lordship of Cemmaes and the castle at Nevern, which they abandoned, favouring nearby Newport as their administrative centre and allowing the double-motted site to decay. (See: 'Nevern Castle: A new interpretation', by Roger Turvey, in *The Journal of the Pembrokeshire Historical Society*, number 3, 1989, pages 57-66, for a more complete discussion of this issue.)

Today, the fine double-motted castle is completely accessible at any reasonable time, free of charge. Nevern Castle is an intriguing site, one of the few substantially rebuilt by the princes of Deheubarth after originating as a Norman stronghold. The impressive monument recalls an age of strife, when the Welsh fought for independence against the Normans and for power amongst themselves.

Newhouse / Castell Coch

Fortified residence
Location: 3 miles west of Narberth (SN 072 136)
Access: Visible (just) from public footpath

Head south on the A4075 from its junction with the A40 at Canaston Bridge. You want to park just before you leave Canaston Wood, a major block of woodland that you soon enter about a mile south of the junction. Take a footpath that is signposted off to the right just inside the far edge of the block of woodland. Keep to the left at all junctions along the footpath, and watch closely for the remains, which are obscured by vegetation and lie in the bottom of the valley on the left.

Known both as Newhouse and Castell Coch (as OS maps identify the site), the ruined rectangular building probably dates to the 14th century; however, who built the fortified dwelling remains a mystery. Set in the remains of a defensive mound in a valley bottom riddled with streams, Newhouse measured 23 by 10.4 metres and had walls over 1.5 metres thick. Clearly, the building was a sturdy structure, intended to provide at least a moderate amount of security for its residents, not just because its walls were thick but also because they were fronted by a rock-cut ditch some 4 metres in depth. When the ditch was added is unclear. Speculation exists that the ivy-clad site also featured a gatehouse at the south-east corner and a rectangular courtyard enclosed by a heavy earthen embankment.

Accessed by an external staircase, the starkly simple hall originally filled the entire first storey; another staircase, located in the south-west corner of the basement, linked the hall to the ground level and also to the roofline. In the 16th or 17th century, a cross-wall was built which blocked off a portion of the eastern side of the hall house. In

Site of the vice, or spiral staircase, that linked the storeys

addition, fireplaces and an upper storey were also added. These additions may have been made by the Barlows of Slebech, who owned Newhouse and much of the surrounding lands.

New Moat

Motte
Location: 10 miles north-east of Haverfordwest (SO 063 253)
Access: Visible from nearby public footpath

To gain access, park by the T-junction of roads in the village centre. Walk a short distance down the lane leading to the church (only its tower dates to the Middle Ages) to a gate with a footpath sign on the left of the road. The motte can be seen in the field here and the footpath passes close by.

Located on a minor road just off the B4313 Fishguard to Narberth road, New Moat (also known as Newmoat and *Nova Mota* in early records) was an important borough under the control of the Bishops of St Davids in the 13th century. Some historians believe that the castle at New Moat may have replaced the one still in existence, but now rapidly being quarried, not too far away at Henry's Moat, and was probably erected prior to the expansion of the manor by the bishops. For a time, the motte may have defended the neighbouring settlement.

The modest 12th-century motte stands in the midst of an open field, surrounded by a partly water-filled ditch and topped with heavy underbrush, bracken and tall grasses. The motte itself is in reasonable condition, and has a so-called 'inverted pudding basin shape' and a flat top. It rises 5.2 metres high and stretches 19.7 metres across at the summit. Traces of a stone-built dam exist on the east side of the moat, but a large tree has damaged and distorted it. The sluice may be a later addition.

A large bailey covering an area of approximately 125 by 80 metres may be seen on the south and western sides of the motte. Hedgerows mark its outer perimeter closest to the road and the original embankments are still identifiable.

Newport / Trefdraeth

Enclosure Castle
Location: (SN 057 388)
Access: Exterior only may be seen

Clear views of the fine stone castle at Newport are obscured by the cottages and other buildings that line the A487, which cuts through the attractive town. Yet, a brief trek off the main road takes visitors directly to the castle, which towers overhead on elevated ground. Even though the medieval castle was long ago incorporated into a later private residence, which is not open to the public, much of the original fabric is visible. To the west of the main structure, a significant section of towered medieval masonry stands on its own alongside the drive to the property (see photo on p.160). Visitors can approach these ruins, but access is limited.

More than likely, this stone castle replaced the earthen ringwork castle that still exists at the northern end of Newport, near the waterfront (see next entry). Having abandoned their castle at Nevern, which was seized by the Welsh in the late 12th century, the FitzMartins, Norman lords of Cemmaes (Cemais), moved their seat to Newport. After the ringwork castle was assaulted, the FitzMartins probably chose to retreat to the hills at the southern end of the new township. They began erecting the masonry stronghold in the 13th century, perhaps shortly after Llywelyn ab Iorwerth wrought havoc in the area in 1215 or after a second Welsh attack, which occurred in 1257, devastated the castle and the town. Along with this castle, the FitzMartins founded a thriving borough and the parish Church of St Mary at its base.

Newport's masonry castle possibly began as a ringwork. Much larger than the one nearer the estuary, this ringwork measured some 55 metres across and was surrounded by a ditch and outer bank, portions of which survive. By the end of the 13th century, the FitzMartins had fortified the site with stone. Much of their stronghold is ruined or incorporated into the later residence, which was added to the property in the late 19th century.

Ownership of the castle passed to James de Audley, nephew of William FitzMartin, upon FitzMartin's death in 1325. In 1497, after James Touchet, Lord Audley and Lord of Cemais, was beheaded for high treason, Newport Castle reverted to the Crown. In 1534, Audley's son regained the lordship of Cemais, and with it, the castle, which remained in the Audley family until 1543, when William Owen of nearby Henllys bought the site. Unfortunately, by the end of the 16th century, the castle had begun to decay. It continued to decline until 1859, when Sir Thomas Lloyd, Baronet of Bronwydd and Lord of Cemais, acquired the property and began its transformation into a private residence.

To best view the medieval remains, one must walk the perimeter of the castle, which can be accomplished but only at road level (where the now in-filled ditch once ran). On the northern side of the imposing hill stand the ruins of the twin-towered gatehouse, one round and the other rectangular, which became an integral part of Sir Thomas Lloyd's 19th century house. At one time, the curtain wall and its massive towers enclosed the entire castle site. Now, west of the main gatehouse only remnants of the wall and its latrines stand alongside the so-called Hunter's Tower (or Hunter's Hall). The D-shaped tower had a pentagonal base and contained the well and a postern gate. Formerly rising three storeys, this tower has almost completely disappeared.

Heading southward around the castle, visitors reach the driveway onto the property, where more medieval remains are visible. Between Hunter's Tower and the lane, a large round tower dominated the south-western angle of the site. Known as the Kitchen Tower, today nothing of substance remains, except for an oubliette measuring 3 by 2 metres, added in the 19th century. The exterior of the south-eastern side of the castle can be viewed, at least from afar, on the right side of the driveway (see photo this page). Closest to the visitor is another D-shaped tower, which still rises two storeys, contains a spiral staircase, has a square base and a latrine accessed from the inner ward. Alongside the tower are the remains of a square structure featuring a rib-vaulted undercroft and a central supportive pier, which suggests usage as

D-shaped tower on south-west side of the castle

a crypt. Only the outer side of this structure is visible to the public.

From the street in the town centre, it is the 19th-century residence that commands attention. Protruding outwards from the northern façade, the remains of the original medieval gatehouse, including one of the two drum towers, dominate the spot. A short distance to the west, fragments of the so-called Hunter's Tower are also visible.

Newport (ringwork)

Ringwork
Location: On the north-east of Newport (SN 058 396)
Access: Freely accessible

While Newport's masonry castle (see previous entry) is better known and dominates the centre of the town, another medieval castle sits close to the Nevern estuary. Now sandwiched between the rugby pitch and the long distance coastal path at the edge of the estuary, the remains primarily consist of a ditch and ringwork on the southern side.

Once classified as an Iron Age defended enclosure, 15th-century documents identify the site as the 'Old Castle'. The ringwork was probably built by William FitzMartin in about 1197 between the two medieval streets, Long Street and St Mary's, that still dominate the town. It may have been built when the FitzMartins abandoned nearby Nevern Castle (see separate entry), whilst the stonework castle on the opposite side of Newport was probably begun in the next century in response to several destructive assaults carried out by the Welsh.

Parc y Castell

Ringwork
Location: Just west of St Davids (SM 744 251)
Access: Visible from the nearby minor road

A fine example of a partial ringwork and bailey survives at St Davids, on the left side of the road to Porth Clais perched above the River Alun, which also flows past the historic medieval cathedral. The massive bank and ditch are overgrown with the normal assortment of vegetation, and enclose an area which measures 27 by 33 metres. Steep natural slopes dropping to the river on the east side provided added defence for both the ringwork and the accompanying rectilinear bailey.

Probably erected by the Bishops of St Davids to defend the early cathedral precinct from attack, the ringwork may date to about 1115, when the Norman Bishop Bernard took over St Davids from the last Welsh bishop.

Parc y Marl

Ringwork or Motte
Location: 10 miles north-east of Haverfordwest (SN 047 245)
Access: Private, not visible from adjacent road

The site is east of the village of Llys-y-Fran and just off the Clarbeston Road, south of Gwastad. Marked on the OS Pathfinder map as a 'homestead' and the Explorer as 'Enclosure', various sources also classify this site as a motte, a ringwork, a defended enclosure and an Iron Age fort. The inner bailey stretches about 60 metres across.

Paterchurch Tower

Fortified Tower
Location: Pembroke Dockyard (SM 957 035)
Access: None, on dockyard premises,
but can be seen over the dockyard wall

Partly hidden by the dockyard wall, vestiges of Paterchurch Tower survive directly opposite the hospital on the northern side of Fort Road, and from where a decent view can be had.

Paterchurch Tower, which may originally have been a tower house similar in design to that at Angle (see separate entry), has long since been engulfed by the spreading shipyard at Pembroke Dock. However, the shell of the three-storey vaulted tower still survives on land that once formed part of the de Paterchurch estate in the Middle Ages. The history of ownership and development of Paterchurch Tower is poorly documented. There is some speculation that the tower belonged to the Knights of St John of Jerusalem (the Hospitallers), who acquired the lands from Gilbert de Clare and established a hospital. They maintained a commandery at Slebech, east of Haverfordwest, the ruins of which survive. Yet historical documents do record the presence of the de Paterchurch (or Patrickchurch) family at least by 1289, and it is reasonable to assume that the fortified tower served as their residence for at least a short period of time.

Standing over 10 metres high and having walls ranging between 1 and just over 2 metres in thickness, the tower was well positioned to watch over the activity on Milford Haven from its southern shores. Each storey contained a single room, measuring about $2^1/_2$ by 3 metres, which offered little in the way of comfort. Each of the upper floors was equipped with a fireplace with flues that rotated clockwise through the two chimneys that projected above the battlemented roofline. Access to the upper storeys was provided by a spiral staircase in a round corner turret, which also survives. Some historians speculate that the fortified tower may actually have served as some sort of lookout post or observation post to warn the garrison at Pembroke Castle of imminent danger. However, this notion remains conjecture.

The Paterchurch estate covered at least 230 acres of prime waterfront property stretching from Pennar Point to Cosheston (Pill?), which was well suited to farming and husbandry. In 1422, the estate passed to John Adam(e)s of Buckspool upon his marriage to Elen (Alson), the daughter of David de Paterchurch. The Adams family occupied the site—and undoubtedly expanded the tower house—until the 17th century, when they found themselves in deep financial straits apparently as a result of losses accrued during the Civil War.

The family's financial problems led to the division of the estates in 1665, after Nicholas Adams married a second time and agreed to a marriage settlement providing for any children. (Adams already had three children from his first marriage to Frances Bowen of Upton Castle.) When his father died in 1685, Rice, the eldest son from Adams' first marriage, inherited not only the Paterchurch estates but also his mounting debts. By this time, additional structures, including a farmhouse and ancillary buildings, stood alongside the medieval tower. The family's dire financial situation lingered well into the 18th century, and Paterchurch passed to Sir Arthur Owen in about 1716, even though the Adams heirs continued to insist they had legal rights to the estate. Then the Meyrick family acquired the Paterchurch estates, and sold Paterchurch Farm to the Board of Ordnance in 1757 and thence it passed to the Admiralty, which began construction of the dockyard in the early 18th century. Pembroke Dock soon engulfed tiny Paterchurch.

Interestingly, work undertaken at the dockyard in 1844 revealed the graves of several skeletons, which were reputedly associated with the owners of the tower. The last recorded burial at the family-owned cemetery was that of Roger Adams, in 1731.

Pembroke

Enclosure Castle
Location: Pembroke (SM 982 016)
Access: Open on most days of the year

In many ways, Pembroke town and castle are outstanding examples of a medieval planted settlement. Perched at the western end of a steep-sided promontory swept on all but its southern side by the tidal waters of the Pembroke River, a tributary of the Milford Haven estuary, the castle dominated the spot. Founded by the Normans, who swiftly laid claim to west Wales immediately after the death of Rhys ap Tewdwr, the Welsh king of Deheubarth, Pembroke Castle grew from a modest but well-positioned earth and timber fortress into one of Wales' mightiest stone castles. Volume II of the Pembrokeshire County History (2001) states that it is likely that it was the Earl of Shrewsbury's son, Arnulf, who headed to Pembroke from Cardigan and established the castle there. Its timber defences easily withstood Welsh attacks during the late 11th century, and the castle only really saw military action during the English Civil War, when it became a focal point for Oliver Cromwell's wrath in 1648.

The triangular inner ward probably reflects the plan of the original earth and timber castle, of which nothing now survives except for traces of a deep ditch (and bank?) which defended the vulnerable inland side of the site. Alongside the ditch, the perimeter of the early castle would have been lined with timber ramparts. Access may have been provided by a simple timber gateway on the western side facing the Benedictine priory, which de Montgomery founded in 1098 across the tidal inlet. Archaeologists have been unable to confirm whether or not a motte once stood at Pembroke; some have speculated that it may have been levelled during the 13th century to make way for the great keep.

After failing to take Pembroke during their revolt in 1094, two years later the Welsh again besieged Pembroke Castle, which was then held by Gerald de Windsor, as constable for de Montgomery. Even though the garrison was on the verge of starvation, the constable managed to deflect the Welsh assault with a shrewd ruse. He first sent a letter to Montgomery claiming he had plenty of supplies and was waiting reinforcements, knowing that the letter would fall into Welsh hands, and then tossed pig carcasses over the curtain walls, implying he had plenty of meat to feed his troops. The ploy worked and—according to Gerald of Wales, de Windsor's descendant—the Welsh retreated.

In 1102, Arnulf de Montgomery and his half-brother, Robert de Belleme, rebelled against King Henry I. When their efforts failed, de Montgomery forfeited his rights to Pembroke Castle. The castle remained Crown property until 1138, when King Stephen appointed Gilbert FitzGilbert de Clare as the first Earl of Pembroke, expecting de Clare to deal with the Welsh threat in his stead. Gilbert's son, Richard FitzGilbert de Clare (also known as 'Strongbow') became Earl of Pembroke in 1148. As the seat of the influential Earls of Pembroke, the castle now became an administrative centre. Strongbow may have constructed the first stone structure at the castle, a simple rectangular building now known as the 'Old Hall' (also called the 'Norman Hall'), the shell of which survives at the eastern corner of the inner ward. Now extensively ruined, the first floor hall may have served as a solar of sorts.

In 1169/70, Strongbow staged his invasion of Ireland from the castle, and recruited many locals to fight along with him. De Clare then remained in Ireland for the last six years of his life, dying in

1176. It was not until 1171 that Henry II officially recognised Strongbow as an earl, but of Striguil (Chepstow) and not of Pembroke. (Strongbow had supported King Stephen against Henry's mother, Matilda.) In the meantime, the English king reasserted his own dominion in West Wales, with the Welsh prince of Deheubarth, Rhys ap Gruffydd, at Pembroke Castle.

William Marshal (the Elder) married Isabel de Clare and was created Earl of Pembroke by King John in 1199. Various commitments, not least service in France, kept Marshal away from Pembroke for five years. But shortly after his arrival in 1204 he began a major rebuilding programme, replacing the timber structures that still remained. Probably inspired by similar designs built by King Philip Augustus in France, Marshal also began his masterpiece, the free-standing domed keep.

The great keep,
with the Horseshoe Gate to the left
and the Dungeon Tower to the rear

Rising some 22 metres and measuring about 16 metres in diameter, the great cylinder still dominates the inner ward. It is unique, not just to Wales but to the rest of Britain as well. Constructed from carboniferous limestone, the walls of the keep remain intact, measuring some 4 metres thick. Originally, the main doorway to the keep was at first floor level, accessed via an external stone stairway, but the entrance was later moved to the basement. A restored spiral staircase rises within the thickness of the walls from ground level to the rooftop of the now floorless keep. On top of the dome-capped tower, visitors will discover expansive views of Pembroke itself and the surrounding countryside.

Notable features include a battered foundation, string-courses, putlog holes, beam holes for timber hoarding, fireplaces on the first and second floors, an ornate window with seats on the second storey, and arrowslits. The third level evidently served as a fighting platform, while the domed vault that covers the rooftop completely contained the fourth floor. The keep is noticeably lacking in sanitary facilities which were provided in several other buildings, including a square latrine turret possibly added by William Marshal in 1211 at the eastern corner of the inner bailey.

Marshal may also have built the simple gatetower that now survives only as horseshoe-shaped foundations cut into limestone bedrock to the west of the great keep. Before the castle's expansion later in the century, this gateway served as the main entrance, quite possibly replacing an earlier timber tower. It measured almost 14 metres in length by 9 metres in width, and had walls at least 2 metres thick. The tower was weakly defended with two pairs of doors, and lacked a portcullis. A small gap on the eastern side indicates that a postern gate may have allowed quick egress when needed. A road would have led to the gate from the town, which was starting to grow to the south-east of the castle, and passed through the spot now guarded by the watergate (built in the later 13th century) before approaching the entrance itself. With the construction of the outer bailey and the towered curtain wall later in the century, not only was a new gatehouse built, but the course of the town road was altered as well. When the entire site was enclosed with a masonry wall, a new watergate blocked the approachway into the Marshal castle.

After William Marshal's death in 1219, his sons (also Earls of Pembroke) continued their father's building programme, not just at Pembroke Castle but also at Cilgerran (see separate entry). While fortifying the inner ward in stone, they also expanded the castle to include the outer ward. More than likely, however, it was not until the appointment of William de Valence as Earl of Pembroke (1247–96) that masonry replaced the timber ramparts, and the castle acquired the form we see today. Ultimately, the Marshal castle occupied what became the inner ward, which was fronted by

Interior of the the Norman Old Hall

the ditch and enclosed, perhaps with a timber palisade, but quite possibly with a stone wall constructed at the same time as the horseshoe gate. This castle contained the great keep, which stood slightly north-east of the D-shaped gatetower, and also featured the Old Hall, and possibly the so-called North Turret, which served latterly as an engine platform.

The Marshals may also have added the buildings at the southwestern corner of the inner ward: the so-called Western Hall and an adjoining rectangular building. Speculation exists that the ruined long building, which runs approximately east-west, may have served as the chapel, but excavations have not substantiated this notion. Extensively restored, the Western Hall features a barrel-vaulted chamber defended on its southern wall with three small arrowslits, one of which also covered the horseshoe gate; a fireplace; and a latrine, which projected outwards from the castle. A spiral staircase gave access to the wall-walk at the rear of the hall, where three individual turrets were located. Access is now restricted.

William Marshal's heirs continued to play a key role in the politics of the times. They fought the Welsh, the Irish in Ireland and the

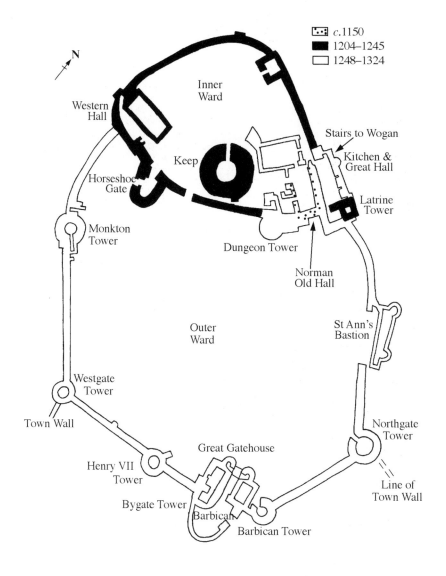

Plan of Pembroke Castle

171

Western Hall

French. Richard Marshal (1231–34) led a small group of barons in a rebellion against Henry III, and for a brief time allied with Llywelyn ab Iorwerth, before sailing to his death in Ireland. Even though Dafydd ap Llywelyn led the Welsh on an extended rebellion throughout Walter Marshal's tenure as Earl of Pembroke (1241–45), Marshal never actually fought the Welshman, and died suddenly from an illness in 1245. His brother, Anselm, who died shortly thereafter, never acquired the earldom, and in 1246, Nicholas de Meules and Robert Walerand gained custodial control of the castles at Pembroke, Haverford, Cilgerran, Tenby, and Narberth, all in Pembrokeshire.

In the following year, the Marshal lands were partitioned between the female heiresses and their husbands. Joan de Muchensey, William Marshal's granddaughter, and her husband, William de Valence (half-brother to the king), received the castles of Tenby and Pembroke. In 1247, de Valence took over the earldom and castle of Pembroke. Even though Henry III never officially recognised de Valence and his wife as Earl and Countess, the two styled themselves as such, and embarked on a major castle-building programme enclosing the outer ward with a towered masonry wall and fronting the castle with a formidable gatehouse and barbican complex (see the photograph at the start of this entry).

One of Britain's first keep-gatehouses, the great gatehouse is an outstanding example of its kind, and contained both heavy defences and comfortable living quarters, at least by the standards of the times. It was probably the first structure de Valence added after he acquired the castle. Access to the outer ward of the castle was evidently first provided by a simple archway, which opened into the barbican. The horseshoe-shaped outwork was little more than a rounded wall, but its purpose was to confine

Entry into the barbican

the enemy in an enclosed space outside the castle itself; from inside the flanking towers, which faced the trapped soldiers, the garrison could fire down upon the enemy without fearing retaliation.

The gate passage contained two portcullises, backed by heavy timber doors secured in place by iron drawbars, and three murder-holes opened in the ceiling. Arrowslits were provided in the round flanking towers on either side of the entryway. Doorways on either side of the passageway gave access to chambers possibly used as guardrooms and also to spiral staircases which reached the upper storeys of the gatehouse and the adjoining Bygate and Barbican towers. The stair turrets project into the outer ward and actually rise to roof level to form two watchtowers. Between the two turrets at the far end of the passage, a two-storey battlemented structure—sometimes called a 'flying penthouse'—stands suspended on a segmental arch. Its purpose is unclear, although Cathcart King has suggested it functioned to protect the gatehouse from attack from inside the castle itself.

The D-shaped Bygate Tower on the western side of the gate-house actually projects outward into the barbican, while the circular Barbican Tower is linked to the south-eastern side of the gatehouse by a short section of curtain wall. Parliamentary forces attempted to destroy both towers during the 1648 siege; the outer façade of the Bygate Tower was almost completely destroyed while the Barbican Tower failed to collapse as intended. Both towers and portions of the gatehouse were rebuilt during J.R. Cobb's restoration programme in the 1880s. The western side of the gatehouse provided access to both levels of the flying penthouse and also to the portcullis chamber. A small passageway led to the wall-walk and also to a garderobe, which retains a fragment of its wooden seat. The basement level of the attached Bygate Tower held a prison.

On the opposite side of the gatehouse, the eastern chamber gave access to the Barbican Tower, which features an aumbry, windows with seats, a fireplace, a garderobe on the first floor, and arrowslits designed to enable archers to fire very close to the base of the tower. A spiral staircase rises to the rooftop, while a doorway on the second floor opens to the wall-walk.

Riddled with mural passages and a well-appointed wall-walk, the substantial curtain wall is pierced by four additional round towers and a rectangular bastion, and two water ports lead to the outside at either side of the castle. These towers date to William de Valence's first building programme at the castle. From the gatehouse, towers along the western curtain wall include the Henry VII Tower, so-called because of its reputation as the king's birthplace (some scholars support the notion that Margaret Beaufort would have found more comfort giving birth in one of the chambers in the gatehouse itself); Westgate Tower, which stands at the junction of two lengths of curtain wall; and Monkton Tower, which overlooks the water port and site of the original pathway into the Norman castle. Beyond Monkton Tower, the curtain wall continues to the south-western corner of the inner ward, where it joins the Western Hall, described above. From the Bastion Tower, the wall-walk progresses northward to intersect with the Northgate Tower, from which a short span of wall-walk merges with St Anne's Bastion, built in the late 13th century. The second postern gate is located at the ground level junction of the two structures.

Like the Bygate Tower, the Henry VII Tower was heavily damaged during the assault on the castle in 1648. The round front was reconstructed during the 19th century restoration project. Much of the interior has been restored as well, and now contains exhibits that reinforce the tradition that Henry VII was born inside the tower. Noteworthy features in this three-storey tower include an arched aumbry in the basement chamber, another aumbry and a fireplace at first floor level, and a fireplace on the second storey. The spiral staircase linking the levels actually consists of two disjoined sections: the lower portion links the entrance passage at basement level to the mural gallery that runs through the curtain wall at the first floor, while the upper section rises from the west side of the first floor and is contained with a projection of walling situated between the tower and the curtain wall. The tower is crowned with a turret, which is accessible from an outside staircase. Another staircase at ground level provides access from the outer ward.

The curtain wall between the Henry VII Tower and Westgate Tower features a mural gallery, and is in excellent condition. About midway along the wall, a short porchway provides stairs into another garderobe. At the western end of this span of wall stands the Westgate Tower, which was extensively restored in the 19th century despite only being damaged on the eastern side in 1648. Much of the fabric of the two-storey tower is modern. The medieval town wall once extended to Westgate Tower, where it merged with the castle.

A doorway on the western side of the Westgate Tower provides access to the curtain wall, which then continues to Monkton Tower, which straddles the wall. So named because it overlooks Monkton Pill and the priory beyond, the round tower rises two storeys. The tower lacks an internal stairway to connect the two levels; the lower level can only be reached via a short set of stairs which descend from the wall-walk, while the upper storey is reachable only by an exterior stairway on the western side of the tower. Inside, Monkton Tower contains a garderobe, barrel-vaulted chambers, an aumbry, and thick plastering still engraved with medieval graffiti, crosses and shields. The first floor features a round-backed fireplace, windows with seats and an arrowslit pointing toward the interior of the castle, perhaps strategically placed to defend the horseshoe gate. The postern gate (or water port) opens in the curtain wall near the base of the tower. It actually consists of two gates: the lower

The Monkton Tower and watergate

View towards the inner bailey from the Monkton Tower

gateway is the older of the two. Beyond the watergate, the curtain wall stretches to the inner ward and crosses the site of the original ditch. Near the farthest end, a garderobe is embedded in the thickness of the wall.

Greatly damaged in 1648, the restored Northgate Tower dominates the curtain wall north of the Barbican Tower, at the eastern corner of the outer bailey, where it once also connected with the medieval town wall. The tower contains several garderobes and a fireplace, and, at its far end, it overlooks another postern gate, sometimes known as the Mill Port.

The skewed position of St Anne's Bastion, which juts outward from the main line of the curtain wall at this point, indicates it was added at a somewhat later date and that the wall originally continued on a straighter path to a point beyond the bastion. Possibly built to plug a gap or weak spot in the defences, the rectangular bastion seems curiously out of place. Two rounded turrets project outward to overlook the river, while a square turret points southwards near the postern gate. The bastion's transformation into a set of modern conveniences has seriously restricted public access to the interior.

A fifth rounded tower, the Dungeon Tower, projects into the ditch that separates the two wards. Also erected by William de Valence, the tower is only accessible from the inner ward. The unusual structure contains three storeys. The lowest level served as the pit prison, entry into which was only afforded via a small trap-door in the floor of the room overhead. An external staircase, much restored, provides access to the first floor, where a spiral staircase continues up to the second storey and the rooftop. At one time, a doorway on the second floor opened onto the wall-walk on the inner curtain wall.

Following temporary exile (1258–61) and the barons' rebellion later in the same decade, de Valence finally returned to Pembroke Castle and added several other buildings to the inner ward. When approaching the maze of structures he created in the eastern corner, the first building one reaches is the court house, also known as the county court or chancery. The large rectangular building is now an empty shell, much of which has been restored. The southern side faces the great keep, and the court house adjoins the Norman Old Hall on the east. At this time, the Earl also built a latrine block alongside the Dungeon Tower, which was only accessible from the Norman Old Hall and projected outward into the inner ditch. On the south-eastern side of the Old Hall, de Valence also added a solar, the first floor of which contained a fireplace and a 'Flemish' chimney, another aumbry, and an oriel window, a later addition.

The most impressive structures added during this second building programme—the great hall and kitchen block—projected outward from the curtain wall on the northern side of the Old Hall. Once topped with battlements, the first floor hall featured dressed stone, large windows with ornate carvings, two aumbreys, and a latrine turret at its north-eastern end. The fireplace in the centre of the southern wall is modern; it may mark the location of its medieval counterpart, and, hence, the kitchen. A squarish building juts into the outer ward at the eastern end of the great hall, where the buttery probably occupied the ground floor. The upper floor adjacent to the latrine turret contained a chamber, the purpose of which is uncertain.

Arguably Pembroke Castle's most intriguing feature can only be reached via the steep spiral staircase at the north-western corner of the great hall—an enormous natural cavern called the 'wogan'. Dripping and slippery, the spot once allowed sailing ships into the castle to dock and unload supplies with relative safety. The river has now receded well away from the mouth of the wogan, which is barred by an iron grate, but visitors can enter the cavern from inside or peer into it while strolling the pathway that encircles the castle.

During the 1270s, de Valence stepped up his service to the king, particularly after his nephew became Edward I, and spent considerable time away from the castle fighting the Welsh and intervening in the affairs of State. He died in England after being mortally wounded in Gascony. His son, Aymer, took over the earldom in 1307 and possibly completed any building works left unfinished at his father's death, including the extensive town walls which it is now believed that William de Valence probably constructed at about the same time as the outer ward received the massive gatehouse and towered curtain wall.

As at Tenby (see separate entry), Pembroke's medieval walls encompassed the whole town, and extensive sections still survive. The masonry walls connected directly to the western and eastern sides of the castle, so that town and castle were one unit. When complete, the circuit featured six round towers (four of which remain) and three gateways, one of which was twin-towered (and no longer survives). Near the castle's West Gate Tower, fragments of the medieval gate are visible, and include a portion of its southern side and springings. At the north-eastern end of the town stood the so-called Round Turret and Barnard's Tower; on the

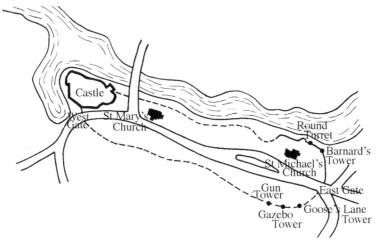

Plan of Pembroke showing the line of the town walls and positions of the gates

south-eastern side stood a round tower known as Goose's Lane Tower (now only a fragment), the so-called Gazebo Tower (the upper half of which has been replaced with a modern structure), and the Gun Tower. Barnard's Tower stands three storeys tall, retains its battlements, although they are in poor condition, and can be accessed from the town wall. Inside at first floor level, the tower contains a garderobe, arrowslits and a portcullis groove. The second storey features a round-backed fireplace, a window and additional arrowslits. A fine section of town wall runs to the south-east of Barnard's Tower.

After the death of Aymer de Valence in 1324, the earldom and castle of Pembroke passed to by right of marriage to Laurence de Hastings and his heirs, who neglected the maintenance of the castle. By the end of the 14th century, the castle was greatly decayed, but still usable. After the death of the last de Hastings heir, John, in 1389, it became the property of the Crown. During the Glyndwr Rebellion, Sir Francis de Court was granted the castles and lordships of Pembroke, Tenby and Cilgerran in exchange for an annual rent of 100 marks. In 1405, the Welsh rebels captured Thomas Roche, the castle's constable, but the castle itself remained in English hands. Upon de Court's death in 1413, King Henry V granted the three castles to his youngest brother, Humphrey, whom he created Duke of Gloucester and Earl of Pembroke in 1414. Following Humphrey's death in 1447, Pembroke Castle passed to William de la Pole, Earl of Suffolk, and then to Margaret, queen to Henry VI.

In 1453, Henry VI appointed his half-brother, Edmund Tudur, as Earl of Richmond and gave him responsibility for Wales, while half-brother Jasper became Earl of Pembroke. During the Wars of the Roses, Jasper Tudur repeatedly fell in and out of favour with the king, but in 1454 he received the castle as part of the earldom of Pembroke. In November 1456 Edmund Tudur died while incarcerated at Carmarthen Castle having been captured nearby by forces loyal to the Duke of York, who feared Tudur might attempt to deprive him of his power base. Three months later his widow, Margaret Beaufort, daughter of the Duke of Somerset and granddaughter of John of Gaunt, gave birth to the future king of England, Harri.

After the Yorkist victories at Mortimer's Cross and Towton, Jasper Tudur lost his hold on Pembroke, and following the Battle of Towton the castle and title, Earl of Pembroke, were granted to William Herbert. In 1470, when the Lancastrians briefly regained power, Jasper in turn regained his rights to the earldom and castle. However, the following year on Edward IV's triumphant return to power at the Battle of Tewkesbury, William Herbert again sat as Earl of Pembroke, and Jasper fled with Harri to France, where they remained in exile for about a decade. In 1483, they returned with the intention of seizing the kingdom, but failed in their initial effort.

Two years later, an undaunted Harri Tudur renewed his quest for the English throne and sailed from France to the shores of Wales. Landing near Dale in Pembrokeshire, Harri Tudor marched to his birthplace, regained control of the castle at Pembroke, and then headed to England to confront Richard III. Crowned Henry VII after his victory at Bosworth, the king restored his uncle Jasper as Earl of Pembroke, which he remained until his death in 1495.

Pembroke Castle remained an active royal stronghold, and King Henry VIII granted the castle to Queen Anne Boleyn, who acted as Marchioness of Pembroke from 1532 until her execution four years later. Even though the castle continued to decay, it played a key role in the English Civil War, when its garrison repeatedly thwarted Oliver Cromwell's efforts to force surrender. After seven weeks of siege, the defenders finally surrendered when offered favourable terms. (For further details see pp. 35-38.) Not surprisingly, Cromwell ordered the castle's immediate slighting, which took place in 1648.

In the 19th century, antiquarian J.R. Cobb began restoration work on the once imposing castle. Then, during the 1920s and 1930s, Major General Sir Ivor Philipps completed a full-scale restoration project, which largely returned the great fortress to its pre-Civil War condition. Today, Pembroke Castle is managed by the Pembroke Castle Trust, and is open for a fee throughout the year.

Picton

Enclosure Castle
Location: 5 miles east of Haverfordwest (SN 011 135)
Access: Privately owned, open for part of the year

Picton Castle is nestled in lush woodland near the River Cleddau, well off the beaten path about five miles east of Haverfordwest. Take the A40 east to the Rhos exit (the castle is signposted) and follow the serene lane to the castle entrance. A plain medieval arch offers entry into the outer courtyard, the cobbled area where a laundry, carpenter's shop, mason's shop, dairy, billiard room, gun room and stables stood. The makeshift mortuary and the old bake-house are open to the public.

For well over 500 years, Picton Castle has been the residence of one of Pembrokeshire's most influential families, the Philipps. The present owner, Jeremy Philipps, continues to reside at the estate, but in a smaller lodge elsewhere on the property. The castle itself is managed by the Picton Castle Trust, which was established in the late 1980s by the then owners, the late Hon. Hanning and the late Lady Marion Philipps.

The first stone castle was built between 1295 and 1308, by Sir John Wogan, Justiciar of Ireland and member of one of medieval

Pembrokeshire's powerful dynasties (the Wogans even had a chapel dedicated to them in St Davids Cathedral). He acquired the estate upon his marriage to a Picton family heiress.

Apparently, Sir John Wogan was so influenced by hall-houses he had seen in Ireland that he wanted something comparable for himself, so, back in Wales, he built a rectangular structure with no inner bailey which was defended at the corners with seven massive round towers. The main entrance, guarded with a portcullis, actually offered access into the undercroft. A curtain wall surrounded the entire site, but not a defensive ditch. Even though the pile was called Picton Castle, its fortifications were relatively slight, and the site is more properly characterised as a fortified residence.

Ownership of Picton Castle passed from the Wogans by right of marriage between Katherine Wogan and her husband, Owain Dwnn of Kidwelly. In the late 15th century, the Dwnn heiress, Jane, married Thomas ap Philip of Cilsant, Carmarthenshire, who served as esquire to the body of Henry VII (Thomas later anglicised his surname to Philipps). Since then, the castle has remained in the hands of the same Philipps family.

Over time, several modifications transformed Picton Castle, and much of the early fabric of the structure, including the curtain wall, was removed. Besides the castle's overall layout, the undercroft, located beneath the great hall, is one of the few places at the site which still exhibits its medieval rib-vaulting.

In 1405, French troops supporting Owain Glyndwr attacked and temporarily held the castle. The castle also saw brief action during the English Civil War, when Sir Richard Philipps garrisoned it for the king. In 1645 it was seized by Parliamentary troops, but unlike so many others in the realm, Picton Castle remained relatively unscathed and the Philipps family retained ownership.

In the late 17th century, the level of the ground outside the main entrance and the doorway above the medieval entry point were elevated by the construction of a raised walkway and terrace. Consequently, the original entrance is now underground and visitors currently enter at first-floor level, between the two eastern-facing towers which open into the hall. During the mid-1700s, the great hall was recreated as a Palladian reception chamber, and a

The western façade of Picton Castle.
(The previous page shows the eastern façade)

circular library was fitted into the tower to the south-east. In 1776, Sir Richard Philipps was created the first Lord Milford. In about 1800, the four-storey battlemented block at the far end of the castle was added by the first Lord Milford. In 1826, Richard Philipps rebuilt the main entrance, using a neo-Norman design, and also added a new stable block. The Lords Milford owned a vast amount of land and other holdings in Pembrokeshire until well into the 20th century. Philipps descendants served as local sheriffs, justices of the peace, lord lieutenants, and members of Parliament. The castle's colourful interiors reflect their owners' former status within Pembrokeshire and British society.

The Picton Castle Trust has done an outstanding job renovating the exterior of the castle, which is presently rendered in a brilliant white.

The original motte castle built by William de Picton in about 1087 still stands on the property, at some distance from the masonry castle. It is detailed on area Ordnance Survey maps, so bring a compass and a good sense of direction if you wish to trek to that site (see following entry).

Picton

Motte
Location: East of Picton Castle (SN 016 135)
Access: On private land, no access

The original castle in Picton Park, located south-east of Haverfordwest near Rhos, was actually a motte and bailey, which overlooked the River Cleddau about half a mile from the later masonry structure (see previous entry). The motte stands about 7 metres high and has a diameter at the top of about 25 metres. There is a ditch around the western half. The motte has been much affected by later construction, initially of a building erected in c.1790, perhaps of a summerhouse or folly belonging to the Philipps family, which collapsed after only some 35 years. This may in part have been due to the tunnel that was erected straight through the motte, of which part remains, which contains a series of shallow niches that perhaps once held statues, as in a grotto. Then, during the Second World War water tanks were erected on the mound to supply the hospital for American servicemen that was established in Picton Castle. The remains of the concrete foundations for these survive.

William de Picton, a supporter of Arnulf de Montgomery (the builder of mighty Pembroke Castle), apparently erected the mound in the late 11th or early 12th century. The site is well chosen, being on the highest ground around with extensive views over the arms of the Cleddau, and across to St. Davids and the Presselli Mountains on a clear day.

Pointz Castle

Motte
Location: 5 miles east of St Davids (SM 830 237)
Access: Visible from the road

Well-disguised behind the buildings at Pointz Castle Farm and the hedgerows that line the A487 near the Brawdy turnoff, Pointz Castle is a substantial motte. Mentioned in 1326 as *Castrum Poncii*, the motte is visible from the roadside. Standing 5.5 metres high and measuring 10 metres across, the castle mound was probably built in the late 12th century by a man named Pons, Ponce, Punchard, or Punch, a tenant of Peter de Leia, Bishop of St Davids from 1176 to 1190. The property became a principal grange for the bishops but the castle itself lost its value to them. The flat-topped summit features an 'inverted pudding basin' shape, and may have supported a timber tower at one time. Excavations in the 19th century unearthed several bronze coins, and an inscribed cross (Early Christian?) was found atop the motte. It has since been incorporated into the adjoining farmhouse.

Puncheston / Castell Mael

Ringwork
Location: 5 miles east of St Davids (SN 009 298)
Access: Visible from the road

This ringwork is located just off the lane on private property not too far from the village school. The site has clearly been spliced by modern construction, namely in the form of a private residence, and the school itself probably stands on the medieval bailey. Yet, the ring-bank is fairly intact and rises some 3 metres.

Roch

Tower House
Location: 6 miles north-west of Haverfordwest (SM 881 212)
Access: Exterior freely visible, self-catering accommodation

Travellers heading along the A487 west of Haverfordwest will easily identify Roch Castle protruding upward from its rocky seat several miles away in the rolling hills not too far east of St Bride's Bay. The D-shaped tower is an attractive sight, and easy to find in the village centre. Clearly, the spot was an ideal location for a castle, for its inhabitants could see for miles, both to the sea and inland. Today, Roch dominates the village at its base. Restored to its medieval splendour, at least partially, it is now available to the public as self-catering accommodation.

Acquiring its name from the volcanic bedrock on which it was built, Roch Castle was traditionally begun in the late 12th or early 13th century by Adam de la Rupe (or de la Roche) whose family accompanied Strongbow (Richard de Clare, Earl of Pembroke) on his invasion of Ireland. Adam de la Roche allegedly had an inordinate fear of snakes, and his dreams predicted his death from a viper

Distant view from the west

bite. Adam therefore chose the rock-laden site for his castle because he believed the added height would protect him from snakes. Ironically, his dreams proved accurate, when a servant unwittingly brought a viper into the castle with a basket of wood. While most historians name Adam as the castle's builder, another possibility is John de la Roche, Adam's grandson, who held the lordship in the 1260s.

Roch Castle functioned for a time as one of the so-called Landsker castles which commanded the unofficial borderland between the Englishry (to the south) and the Welshry (to the north).

Originally accessed at first-floor level, the battlemented tower house rises three stories. Each of the upper storeys contained a single large chamber with a fireplace, and the hall connected to another chamber which led into what may have been a chapel or an oratory. A rectangular turret containing several small vaulted rooms projects from the rounded side of the apsidal structure. Traces of an embankment and ditch from what may have been the bailey exist on the castle's southern side. There is some speculation that other buildings were planned but never built.

The de la Roche family owned the castle until about 1420, when Thomas de la Roche died without a male heir. The lordship and castle then passed to Edmund, Lord Ferrers, and Sir George Longueville (or Langueville), by right of marriage to the de la Roche heiresses, Eleanor and Elizabeth. Later in the 15th century, the castle was 'modernised' with mullioned windows. In 1601, William Walter of Trefran purchased Roch Castle. William's best known descendant was Lucy Walter, who became King Charles II's mistress and mother of his illegitimate son, James, the future Duke of Monmouth, in 1648.

During the Civil War, the Earl of Carbery (a kinsman of the Walters family) garrisoned Roch Castle for the Royalist cause. When Parliamentarian troops led by Rowland Laugharne captured the castle in 1644, Lucy Walter fled to London for safety, and it was there that she met the future king. Sir Charles Gerard retook the castle a few months later, and the Royalists kept control until 1645, when Cromwell's men seized the castle for the last time. They may have burned the structure to the point that it was no longer usable.

In the late 18th century, John Harries, Esq., of Trefacwn bought the crumbling castle but promptly sold it to John Rhys (Rees) Stokes of Cuffern (Cyfern). In 1899, the Stokes family sold the ruin to John Wynford Philipps, who became the 1st Viscount St Davids early in the next century. By 1900 the castle was a ruin and the present structure was completely restored by the Viscount. Of the original structure, only a portion of the outside walls date back to about 1200, but the interior follows the original floor pattern and much of the castle's medieval integrity remains intact. In 1954, his heir, the 3rd Viscount, sold Roch Castle to Lord Kenswood, who in turn sold the property in 1965 to an American industrialist. The Berry family purchased Roch Castle in 1972 and lease it out as self-catering accommodation upon prior booking.

Rudbaxton

Motte
Location: 3 miles north of Haverfordwest (SM 961 205)
Access: Visible from nearby road

The village and its motte lie just to the east of the A40, 3 miles north of Haverfordwest. Also referred to as Great Rudbaxton to distinguish the site from Rudbaxton Rath, the 4 metre high motte is partly disguised under some trees adjacent to the parish Church of St Michael. Alexander de Rudebac (Rudepac), the first Norman settler in the immediate area, founded the motte and bailey castle in the late 12th or early 13th century, and probably gave his surname to the village. The low, squat mound stretches almost 12 metres across at the summit.

Dating to the 12th century but largely restored in the 1800s, St. Michael's Church contains the unusual Howard monument which lines the eastern side of the lady chapel. Dating to the 17th century, the colourfully painted memorial features nearly life-sized effigies of members of the Howard family grasping several skulls, a grim reminder of the impact of the plague in the region. A red mark on the breast of Thomas Howard reputedly symbolises his untimely death during a duel held on top of the motte.

Rudbaxton Rath / The Rath

Ringwork
Location: 3 miles north-east of Haverfordwest (SM 985 188)
Access: Visible from roadside and via public footpath

From Clarbeston Road, take the lane that leads towards Haverfordwest. Once the road has crossed the bridge over the river at New Bridge, it climbs uphill and when the road bends slightly left having emerged from its wooded climb, you want to park near the field entranceway on the left and opposite a farm track on the right. A public footpath leads through the field gate on the left and alongside the hedge on your right to a stile on to the castle site. The footpath itself only goes about as far as a well found on the northern flank of the ringwork.

Identified on OS maps as 'the Rath', the enormous earthwork perched on sloping farmland just east of the minor road running north-easterly between Crundale and New Bridge is quite visible from the roadside. Why the site has acquired the forename Rudbaxton is not clear, as the village of Rudbaxton lies several miles to the west. Nonetheless, the Rath is an interesting site which probably began its existence as an Iron Age hillfort. Agricultural and pastoral usage has eroded much of the interior and trash has been dumped in parts, but the massive ramparts are still easy to trace. The medieval castle was probably a ringwork, which made shrewd use of the prehistoric ramparts. A small holy well is located near the entrance to the site.

St Davids Palace

Bishop's Palace
Location: Adjacent to the cathedral in St Davids (SM 750 255)
Access: In care of Cadw and open to the public

As a grand residence fit for powerful, albeit ecclesiastical, occupants, the palace may have been the logical replacement for the small ringwork, Parc y Castell, which stood on a hillside nearby (see separate entry). Built in the shadow of the cathedral on the opposite bank of the trickling River Alun, the bishop's palace is now a complex of ruins, whereas the great cathedral remains in outstanding condition and the Bishops of St Davids live elsewhere. In its heyday, however, the palace was a sight to behold, one that the bishops progressively embellished over time. Ultimately, they transformed the simple residence into a palatial masterpiece, the only one of its kind in Pembrokeshire.

Even before the Normans established themselves in west Wales, a religious community existed at St Davids. Founded during the 'Age of the Saints' by Dewi Sant, the settlement revolved around a group of ascetic monks who devoted their lives to relative poverty and scholarly pursuits. The native Welsh princes were well acquainted with St Davids, which was the seat of Bishop Sulien—a Welshman—in the late 11th century. When William I visited St Davids in 1081, not only did he meet with Rhys ap Tewdwr, the king of Deheubarth, he also had an audience with the bishop, who probably acknowledged the king's piety for undertaking the pilgrimage.

In 1115, the Normans replaced the Welsh bishop with their own man, Bernard, who had been serving as Queen Matilda's chaplain. Bishop Bernard is responsible for beginning the palace we see today. However, most of the focus of construction during the 12th and 13th centuries was on the grand cathedral, and slow progress was made on the new palace. Quite possibly, the ringwork castle served as the primary residence for the bishops until the late 12th or early 13th centuries. The early bishops entertained a variety of dignitaries at St Davids. King Henry II visited Bishop David FitzGerald (Gerald of Wales's uncle—see entry on Manorbier Castle) in 1171 and again in 1172. Sixteen years later, Baldwin, the Archbishop of Canterbury, stopped at the palace during his journey around Wales with Gerald of Wales seeking converts for the Third Crusade. These guests may have stayed at the ringwork castle, but the specific location was not documented.

Little remains from the earliest building phase at the palace. Of the complex, only the western range survives, itself the most severely ruined section of the palace. It originally consisted of a single-storey structure, but in the 14th century two barrel-vaulted undercrofts were added at ground level, one of which contained the well. Two narrow rooms filled the upper level, each with its own fireplace, set back to back with a cross-wall connecting them. At the southernmost end, which held a latrine, the western range linked to the great chapel (see photograph at start of this entry), part of Bishop Gower's grandiose 14th-century building programme.

On the northern side of the complex stood a simple, albeit battlemented, gatehouse, which presently serves as the main entrance, and a length of battlemented curtain wall. Both features may date to the tenure of Thomas Bek as Bishop of St Davids (1280–93). The three-storey gatehouse offered access to the palace via a simple archway, and whether the battlements were intended for use by soldiers to defend the palace from an attack is uncertain, but they would at least have presented an image of a fortified structure poised for defence.

The curtain wall itself actually formed a portion of the precinct wall, which continued southwards but turned at right angles as it approached the River Alun. The wall not only enclosed the palace buildings but also surrounded the gardens and orchards on the land just outside the south and eastern ranges. It also linked with the longer, battlemented Cathedral Close wall, which encompassed the palace, the cathedral and canons' houses in an area of some 16 acres. Lengthy expanses of this wall, which Bishop Bek began in 1287, survive around much of the close, which linked to four gateways and at least one corner tower: Porth Gwyn allowed access for travellers from Ireland; Porth Padrig from the seaside at Porth Clais; Porth Boning offered access to land travellers from the north; and the recently restored Porth y Twr welcomed travellers making their way to St Davids from across southern Wales. Bek also founded hospitals in St Davids and Llawhaden, near the bishops castle (see separate entry), a collegiate church at Llanddewi Brefi (in Ceredigion) and another college at Abergwili (Carmarthenshire). Bek's successor, Bishop David Martyn (1290–1327) apparently concentrated on improvements to the cathedral, and added the ornate Lady Chapel to the east side.

Porth y Twr

Bishop Martyn's successor, Henry de Gower (1328–47), spared no expense when it came to remodelling the palace, and most of what survives today dates to his term at St Davids. To the left as one enters the gatehouse stand the ruins of Gower's eastern range, which was completed in two phases. The first structures included the solar and bishop's hall, which run parallel to the western range across the courtyard, and also the east wing, a rectangular building projecting almost at a right angle outwards from the solar. The range is crowned with the spectacular arcading now generally associated with Bishop Gower, which was originally highlighted with checkerboard decoration and is now partly restored.

Today, the extensively ruined condition of this range makes it difficult to imagine its original appearance. The square solar featured a large fireplace, latrine and two large windows, which are now partly blocked, and a small doorway, which allowed servants to enter the chamber as needed. Fronted by a grandiose porch,

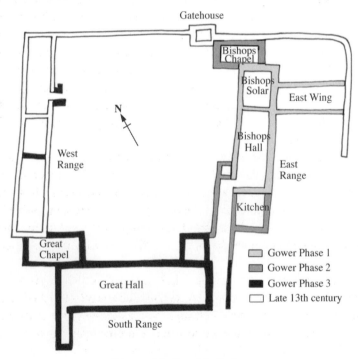

Plan of St Davids Palace

Eastern range with Close wall

which offered access through an ornate semi-octagonal doorway, the lavish bishop's hall stands at the southern end of the solar. Well lit with several tall windows with seats and decorated with human-headed corbels, the bishop's hall once featured a wooden screen that isolated the southernmost end from the rest of the chamber. A spiral staircase at this end gave access to the narrow battlements and also to ground level. A small niche is located about midway up the staircase. Another staircase was secreted inside a corner turret, which offered access to the roof and provided grand views of the cathedral close.

Although the east wing is situated adjacent to the solar, it was accessible from the dais end of the bishop's hall. The upper storey featured a fine fireplace, a latrine (which emptied into a pit at the base of a chimney-like chute) and a large window, and probably served as the bishop's bedroom. Interestingly, the roofline features blind arches rather than the open arcades that trim the solar and bishop's hall.

The porch into the bishop's hall dates to the last phase of Gower's building programme. A rectangular chapel furnished with fully glazed windows was built into the area between the solar and the gatehouse, and at the same time, a narrow passageway was added immediately to the south of the porch. A fairly simple structure, the first floor of the chapel was entered up a set of steps from

Bishops' Hall porch

the courtyard, and featured an enormous archway that served both as a window and a doorway. The new passage connected the east range with the even more impressive south range, constructed during the second phase of construction, and also to the kitchen, which replaced an earlier kitchen that originally continued around the southern end of the bishop's hall. Gower's kitchen featured three ground level vaults and cone-shaped vaults on the first floor, the tops of which culminated in chimneys that drew smoke and heat upwards away from the cooking area. The kitchen was equipped with cupboards and had windows on the east and southern sides. It also provided access to a huge porch, which opened into the great hall, the showpiece of the southern range.

Clearly, the southern range emphasised the wealth and status of the Bishops of St Davids, and that of Bishop Gower in particular. The main entrance to this block—the great porch—immediately grips one's attention upon entering the courtyard. In its original form, the porch would have been the most elaborate structure in the palace. Today, despite its ruinous condition, it still reflects its earlier splendour. Of particular note, the two niches over the archway contain seated carved figures, purported to be King Edward III and his queen, Philippa. Visitors would have been

200

stunned by the bold colours displayed on the porch, its yellow and purple checkerboard arcading embellished with figure corbels and floral designs and also brilliant red painting covering the exterior façade. Not surprisingly, the lavish porch forecast an even greater experience inside.

The great hall served the ceremonial needs of the Bishops of St Davids, who entertained dignitaries and other guests of importance. Now little more than a shell of the original structure, the first floor hall measured about 27 by 9 metres. It was open to the roofline, which stood about 12.5 metres above ground level. Along the northern wall, three tall, glazed windows with seats overlooked the courtyard, while only one window lit the hall on the opposite wall. Bishop Gower's famous arches dominated the wall tops. The dais end was located on the western side of the hall, from where diners could admire the fine rose window, which is remarkably well preserved and one of the highlights of the palace. Cut in Bath stone and set within a circle of carved Caerbwdy sandstone, the skilfully carved window features a central quatrefoil, from which 16 'daggers' radiate outwards. None of the painted glass panes survive.

View from the great chapel towards the cathedral,
with the south range in the foreground, and the eastern range
and main gate at the rear of the palace

Below the grand window, doorways provided access to the kitchen and to six vaulted undercrofts, which held the buttery, storage cellars and a lockable storeroom. Designed with convenience in mind, the two staircases provided servants with access to the upper level—one for climbing upwards, the other to proceed back down to the basement. A well-appointed wooden screen hid the commotion caused by the servants moving between the two levels.

At the west end of the great hall, visitors could retreat into the great chamber, which was separated from the hall by a cross-wall, only the slim foundations of which still exist. The chamber was lit by three windows, one in each wall, while a fireplace occupied a portion of the cross-wall. On the south-western end, a doorway led into a compact latrine block, which emptied into a cesspit. Access to the wall-walk was possible through the same doorway. Small turrets at the end of the chamber had staircases leading to the rooftop.

The great chapel stood on the northern side of the great chamber, situated between the south and western ranges. Prior to the addition of a modest porch some time after the death of Bishop Gower, the impressive structure could only be entered from the great chamber. Lavishly decorated with an elegantly carved and painted sandstone piscina, and equipped with a drainage hole, niches for statues, and glazed windows, the great chapel served the needs of important guests who were rung to mass by two bells located in the small belfry perched on the western wall. As elsewhere in the palace, the chapel was adorned with arcading; traces of battlements also survive.

Besides revamping the bishop's palace, Bishop Gower also left his mark inside St Davids Cathedral (where his mutilated tomb is secured behind the stone pulpitum screen he had constructed prior to his death). He also restored Thomas Bek's close wall and left his architectural input at Lamphey Palace, near Pembroke (see separate entry). After Gower's death, the bishops primarily acted as absentee lords, devoting their attention to other commitments away from St Davids, to where they returned mainly to celebrate the major feast days.

Consequently, the palace began to suffer from neglect, and when William Barlow took over as the first Protestant Bishop of St Davids in 1536, he implemented changes that forever altered the palace. Favouring Abergwili as the primary residence for the Bishops of St Davids, Barlow apparently pulled down the roofing covering the southern range, which exposed the building to the elements. By the early 17th century, the palace had substantially decayed, and a licence for its demolition was granted by the archbishop in 1616. The project never took place, and minor repairs were made by Bishop William Laud in about 1622, when he stayed at the palace. Theophilus Field (1627–35) was the last bishop to use the palace, when he held a chapter meeting in 1633.

Historical documents record the complete ruination of St Davids Bishops Palace by 1670, and permission to demolish the site was again granted in 1678. But as before, the decree was not carried out, and the palace became the home of several local families who built cottages within its walls. During the 19th century restoration project at the cathedral, an attempt was also made to restore the palace. However, little was achieved. Fortunately, in 1932, the palace ruins passed into the care of the State, and the close wall attained State guardianship in the 1940s.

Today, the site is managed by Cadw, which spearheaded a major conservation programme during the 1990s and early 21st century. The Bishops of St Davids still reside at their palace in Abergwili, near Carmarthen.

St Ishmaels

Motte
Location: 5 miles west of Milford Haven (SM 835 076)
Access: Visible from road; ask at cottage for permission to visit

The motte lies on private property behind a cottage on the north side of the village of the same name. Rising some 20 metres, the castle is clearly visible despite being overgrown, and if you wish to visit it, please ask the residents of the cottage—and be prepared for a clamber through thick gorse and bracken. During the Middle Ages, St Ishmaels was an outlying manor of the barony of Walwyn's Castle (see separate entry).

Templeton / Sentence Castle

Ringwork or Motte
Location: 2 miles south of Narberth (SN 110 116)
Access: A public footpath leads onto the site

On the western edge of the village along the A4115 a public footpath is signposted north by a vehicle repair centre / garage. If you
follow this path for a few hundred yards it will lead you on to the
castle mound.

The earthwork castle at Templeton consists of a medium sized
motte with evidence of a ringwork, with the remains of a deep moat
on the north-west. Once thought to have been the predecessor to
Narberth Castle (see separate entry), some historians speculated
that the first reference to Sentence Castle may be in 1116, when
tales in *The Mabinogion* claim the Welsh destroyed a castle in
'Arberth'. However, recent revisions in thinking about the history
of Narberth Castle indicate that the earthwork castle at Templeton
had its own, quite separate history and that 'Arberth Castle' directly
refers to the first castle at nearby Narberth.

Although the Welsh reputedly seized Templeton Castle in 1215,
it was another four years before Llywelyn ab Iorwerth torched the

site and rendered it completely useless. Afterwards, the site disappeared from the historical record. At one time, the ramparts would have risen at least 6 metres and enclosed an inner bailey stretching some 9 metres across. An encircling ditch defended the site. The village itself (*Villa Templarii*) is named for the Knights Templar, who established a hospice there in the late 13th century.

Tenby

Enclosure Castle
Location: Above the harbour, Tenby (SN 138 005)
Access: Freely accessible at all times

While not the only walled town in medieval Pembrokeshire, Tenby is particularly notable for the fine circuit of towered walls that still encloses much of the town, which is known in Welsh as Dynbych y Pysgod, or 'Little Fort of the Fishes', to distinguish it from Denbigh, another walled castle town in North Wales. Probably begun by William de Valence, Earl of Pembroke, in the 13th century, the town walls remain in remarkably good condition, considering their age, the growth of the sprawling market town both within and outside the walls, and the fact that the associated castle is almost completely ruined on the headlands projecting out into Carmarthen Bay on the eastern side of town. Together, however, the medieval walls and castle (and also the narrow lanes, other medieval structures and St Mary's Church in the centre of it all) present a startlingly evocative impression of what Tenby may have looked like in much earlier times.

Although little is known of Tenby's historical origins, a 9th-century poet apparently wrote of a fortress at the spot. If an early medieval fortification did stand here, nothing survives. Nor does anything of the original Norman castle that probably crowned Castle Hill in the 12th century. The Flemings settled in Tenby in about 1111, and for a short time established themselves as cloth-workers. Possession of the early, probably earth and timber, castle fluctuated between the Normans and the Welsh princes of Deheubarth, who, in an assault led by Rhys and Maredudd ap Gruffydd, captured the castle in 1153 in retaliation for the serious wounding of their brother, Cadell, two years earlier. The Normans regained control of the castle shortly thereafter, and it took another 34 years for the Welsh to again attack Tenby and its castle. This time, Maelgwyn ap Rhys and his comrades devastated both town and castle. Once again, the Normans rebuilt the castle, but evidently it was not for another century that the structure was strengthened with masonry defences.

The surviving masonry at Tenby Castle dates to the late 13th century and was probably added after an onslaught by Llywelyn ap Gruffydd, Prince of Gwynedd, and his men in 1260. The town walls were probably built at the same time to further protect Tenby from the Welsh. Almost completely cut off from the mainland, the promontory site actually links to the shoreline by a narrow isthmus of land, which is now well-disguised behind more recent buildings. The site evidently required stronger defences on the landward side, where fragments of a gatetower (said to resemble the great five-arched tower located

The watchtower on Castle Hill

Castle Hill with watchtower and statue of Prince Albert

on the opposite side of the town), a D-shaped barbican and portions of the battlemented curtain wall survive. The Tenby Museum actually incorporates a length of medieval masonry, which may have been part of the great hall.

Devoting more attention and money to the walls over succeeding years, the townspeople began to neglect the castle, which in essence stood outside the confines of the town. For a time, Tenby Castle served an ancillary role as a barracks and a storage facility. Still the property of the earldom of Pembroke, when the lordship passed to John de Hastings, then in his minority, King Richard II made Sir William Beauchamp the royal custodian in 1378. Beauchamp neglected the castle to the point that, within eight years, it reportedly had decaying gates, crumbling curtain walls and severe rot in the lord's chamber due to the removal of the lead roof.

On the summit of Castle Hill, a statue honouring Prince Albert stands near the slender ruins of what is believed to have been a watch tower rather than a residential structure. Speculation exists that the tower, actually composed of two smaller round towers, was a lighthouse. The structure is not accessible to the public. Just west of the tower lie foundations of other buildings, the functions of which are unknown. A 19th-century walkway still circles Castle

Hill; fashionable resort visitors once promenaded around the waterfront showing off their Sunday best and rejuvenating themselves in a luxurious bathhouse, the Laston House, built by Sir William Paxton, which still overlooks the harbour.

The quay was begun in 1328, when Edward III granted Tenby the right to levy taxes to pay for its construction. A portion of the murage tolls probably also paid for repairs to the town walls, which were strengthened in about 1377 in anticipation of invasion by the French. Tenby over time developed into a significant maritime and commercial trading centre, as structures like the Tudor Merchant's House (National Trust) on Quay Hill demonstrate.

In the early 15th century, Tenby and its castle resisted an assault by French troops supporting Owain Glyndwr. Later that same century, Jasper Tudur, Earl of Pembroke and uncle to King Henry VII, signed a Letters Patent turning over the maintenance of Tenby's defences to the mayor and burgesses in perpetuity. The earl apparently also agreed to pay half of the cost of refurbishing the then-decaying castle, which included cleaning out and adding about 9 metres to the ditch outside the town walls along what is now St Florence Parade. The agreement also dealt with construction of new towers, heightening of the walls by 3 metres and embedding new arrowslits at wall-walk level. In 1588, Queen Elizabeth I ordered the town's walls strengthened again, this time to withstand an assault by the Spanish Armada, which never materialised.

Tenby initially supported the Parliamentarian cause during the first English Civil War. In 1642, the town's mayor, David Hammond, and his associate, Devereux Wyatt, readied the town for an assault by Royalist troops. They refortified the castle and town walls, repaired the gateways and gathered enough supplies to withstand a protracted siege. In 1643, the Royalists, led by Richard Vaughan, Earl of Carbery, finally stormed Tenby and seized the castle, which they immediately garrisoned for the king. They managed to hold Tenby until the following year, when Parliamentary troops attacked the town by sea and by land. Although able to thwart the seaward attack, the residents of Royalist Tenby succumbed to the intensive three-day onslaught conducted by their Parliamentary foes, and their leader, Colonel

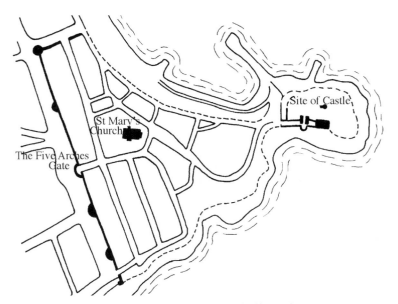

Plan of Tenby showing the town walls and gateways

Rowland Laugharne. Cannon fire seriously damaged the town walls, and some 300 of Charles I's supporters were captured.

Later in the same year, Laugharne and his troops were forced to retreat to the confines of Pembroke Castle, the main Parliamentarian stronghold in Pembrokeshire. After becoming frustrated with the Parliamentary cause and Parliament's intentional underpayment of troops in 1647, Laugharne and his comrade, Colonel John Poyer, military governor of Pembroke Castle, switched their allegiance to the king. During the absence of their own governor, Colonel Rice Powell, the Tenby Castle garrison also turned Royalist. Their actions prompted yet another confrontation with Parliamentary troops, now personally commanded by Oliver Cromwell. In late May 1648, Tenby surrendered to Cromwell after a six-day siege. The fates of Colonels Laugharne, Poyer, and Powell were determined after the siege of Pembroke Castle (see p.ADD).

Tenby's walls are, undeniably, its finest medieval feature. Saved from ruin in 1873 when a local man named Dr Charter obtained an injunction to prevent the town corporation from pulling them down,

Five Arches on the medieval town walls

they date to the late 13th century but have been revamped several times. The stone walls completely ringed the town, except for an area along the southern waterfront which had its own natural defences that were reinforced with masonry at several places. Archaeological evidence indicates that a bank and ditch probably fronted the original, weakly constructed town walls, which were replaced after the Welsh devastated Tenby in 1260.

The strong expanse of battlemented masonry was defended at intervals by several rounded towers and four main gateways, each equipped with a portcullis. Of these, only one gate and seven towers still dominate the western wall. The most elaborate and largest of these massive towers, known locally as the Five Arches or St George's Gate, still stands in excellent condition. Essentially a D-shaped barbican defended with arrowslits, only the north-facing arch is original; the other arches were added in the 19th century. Standing inside the town walls and looking outward toward the gate, it is easy to identify a set of steps leading from the wall-walk adjacent to the Five Arches which allowed access to the portcullis mechanism, situated above the gateway. To the south of this gateway, three smaller wall towers still stand, two of which are round and the third, located between them, is rectangular (it may be a later addition).

The other gateways into Tenby were demolished between 1781 and 1811, upon the orders of the local authorities. By 1784, the town had declined so much that pigs scavenged the squalid streets. In 1792, the North (or Carmarthen) Gate was torn down and replaced later with the Red Lion Hotel, which still marks the end of High Street. Shortly afterwards, the East Gate (Whitesand Gate) and Quay Gate were also destroyed. In 1797, the centre of town was described as completely ruined.

With the turn of the century and the influx of people like Sir William Paxton, Tenby experienced a renaissance and became known for its restorative powers and seaside setting. Today, the town retains much of its medieval integrity, even though many of the buildings are Georgian in style and house modern shops, restaurants and pubs.

Upton

Enclosure Castle / Fortified House
Location: 2 miles north-west of Carew (SN 020 047)
Access: Privately owned, limited opening April to October

Upton Castle can be reached by taking the A477 west just past Carew Cheriton and then turning quickly onto the minor lane leading northwesterly at Milton. Follow that road about one mile and turn northward onto the lane signposted for the castle and gardens. Today, Upton Castle is a private residence; only the surrounding gardens and the 14th-century chapel, built by the Malefants for use as a mausoleum, are accessible to the public. Frustratingly, little is visible of the original medieval castle built in the 13th century that stood in the woodland on a ridge overlooking the Carew River. If visitors are careful, though, they can view glimpses of the exterior of the 'castle', which was extensively rebuilt in the 19th century.

In the late 13th century, Walter Malefant (Malephant, Maliphant) acquired the property and erected the first castle at the site, which was also known as Ockenston and Ucton. The battlemented structure enclosed a central courtyard and featured a north-facing, rectangular hall-block measuring 8 by 4 metres. The hall was situated on the second storey. Round towers flanked the main

One of the castle's surviving round towers

gate passage and a smaller round tower contained a spiral staircase.

In the 15th century, the castle passed by right of marriage from Alice, the Malefant heiress, to Owain ap Gruffydd ap Nicholas of Dinefwr. Their descendants took the surname Bowen and held Upton Castle until the 18th century, when they sold it to John Tasker. Upon Tasker's death, his niece and her husband, Reverend William Evans, inherited the castle. In 1927, their descendants in turn sold the castle to Stanley Neale. Upton Castle is presently owned by the Skeltons, and surrounding gardens are maintained by the Pembrokeshire Coast National Park Authority. Restored in the 1970s, the small chapel, which contains several Malefant family effigies, is open to the public.

Walwyn's Castle

Motte / Ringwork
Location: 4 miles north-west of Milford Haven (SM 873 110)
Access: Can be seen from adjoining churchyard

Overlooking broad vistas and lush farmland, Walwyn's Castle is a huge, undulating motte and bailey castle, located behind the Church of St James. More than likely, the earthworks originally enclosed an Iron Age hillfort, the inner embankment of which was heightened for the 6-metre high motte. A separate bank and ditch was constructed to form a small inner bailey. A few stones still scatter the top of the motte, suggesting that a masonry structure may have stood on the summit, which stretched 18 metres across. Associations with Arthurian legend for a time led to its identification as a burial mound. However, the earthwork castle actually formed part of the same lordship as Laugharne Castle in Carmarthenshire, which in the 13th century was in the possession of the de Brian family of Devon. CARN, the site database of the RCAHMW, has also listed the site as a medieval trading centre. The name Walwyn may refer to a Fleming who settled the area in the 12th century

West Tarr

Possible Tower House
Location: 2½ miles west of Tenby (SN 089 008)
Access: Private

Like its larger but less complete neighbour at Carswell (see separate entry), West Tarr was probably a late medieval yeoman's house. Unlike Carswell, the defensible nature of this small building is questionable, despite having access at first floor level, for it is set back on a steeply sloping hillside and would probably have been easy to seize. Associated with Carswell since 1324 when it was known as Torre or Tarr, the two-storey building at West Tarr features a barrel vaulted undercroft and a vaulted upper level, which may have once supported a vaulted ceiling but but presently is roofed with slate. A staircase offered access between the two storeys. The building features a lateral chimney, which is extensively damaged. A small hearth and flue were added later.

Wiston

Motte and Shell Keep
Location: 4 miles north-east of Haverfordwest (SN 022 181)
Access: In care of Cadw, freely accessible

Wiston Castle is located in the village of Wiston, 4 miles north-east of Haverfordwest, itself best reached from the A40 by taking the signposted road northwards. At the south side of the bailey, the charming parish church of St. Mary provides the perfect landmark for visitors seeking out the medieval stronghold. Park in the church car park and cross the road to the castle entrance.

Wiston Castle is an outstanding example of a motte and bailey castle, and certainly one of the best preserved in Wales. Today, Wiston's substantial motte stands at the northern end of the bailey, rising over 9 metres above the bottom of the ditch while covering over 58 metres at its base and 18 metres in diameter on the flat-topped summit. The mound is still encircled by a 3 metre deep dry ditch now spanned by a small bridge at the western side. Visitors are able to scale the side of the motte using a new series of concrete steps set into the earth during recent restoration efforts undertaken by Cadw.

Perched on top of the mound are the ragged remains of the Norman shell keep which replaced a timber version in the late 12th century or early 13th century, probably to contend with the ever-present threat of assault by the Welsh. Cadw has cleared the gorse and bracken from the sides of the motte and the interior of the keep, an action which has enabled visitors to get a realistic impression of the structure's original design. Interestingly, this shell keep was the only one of its type to be built in Pembrokeshire.

The interior of the keep appears circular, but its external plan was actually 18-sided. The walls average about 3.6 metres in height and measure up to 3 metres in width. Much of the northern wall has fallen towards the ditch, but the arched stonework still preserves details like the holes for the drawbar which secured the gateway and kept out intruders. When complete, the keep would have contained a variety of timber buildings, which no longer survive. Recent excavations revealed the remains of a cross-wall or stone partition between the northward facing chambers.

From atop the motte, the overall plan of the castle is easy to identify. The elliptical bailey adjoining the motte was created by an extensive earthen embankment and associated ditch, which is now mainly visible on the north and western sides. The earthworks enclosed an area of approximately two and a half acres, and probably date to the early 13th century. A drawbridge probably spanned the gap between the bank and the motte. The bailey apparently held the main residence for the lord of the castle, and other buildings vital to the castle's daily administration. Built of timber, they no longer survive.

Wiston Castle was first mentioned in historical records in about 1147, when the Welsh, led by Cadell, Maredudd and Rhys, the sons of Gruffydd ap Rhys ap Tewdwr, stormed the motte and bailey stronghold, but required assistance from Hywel ab Owain to bring the walls down. However, the earth and timber castle probably dates from the start of the 12th century, when its first owner, Wizo (Gwys in Welsh), settled the land, having received the Lordship of Daugleddau from Henry I. Wizo was a Flemish settler, one of scores brought into Wales by the king. His settlement became known as Wizo's town, or Wiston.

When Wizo died in 1130, the earth and timber castle passed to a descendant and then to the Welsh in 1147. Shortly thereafter, the Flemish owners regained control of the castle and held it until 1193, when Hywel Sais, son of the formidable Lord Rhys, attacked the castle and captured Philip FitzWizo and his family. The Welsh prince held the castle for two years before the Normans recaptured it.

Llywelyn ab Iorwerth stormed Wiston Castle in 1220, destroying both town and castle. Though Henry III apparently ordered the people to assist William Marshal, Earl of Pembroke, in the castle's reconstruction, Wiston was abandoned, perhaps in favour of neighbouring Picton. In the meantime Marshal acted as the guardian for an heiress to the Fleming fortunes at Wiston. When the girl grew up she married Sir Walter de Herford, who retained control of the castle by right of marriage. By the 14th century, the motte castle had become part of the extensive holdings of the Wogans of Picton, after another heiress married into the influential family.

Wiston next appears in history in connection with the English Civil War of the 1640s. In 1643, the Royalists stationed a small outpost of men at Wiston, possibly on the bailey grounds. When Parliamentary forces attacked Royalist encampments during the following year, the men at Wiston quietly surrendered. Wiston may have been the Parliamentarian army's staging point on their march to Colby Moor where they defeated the Royalists (see also pp.36-37).

After the Civil War, Wizo's castle became part of a farm and the property was used for grazing. The castle itself saw no further action, except for consolidation work in the 20th century and the normal activities expected of cattle that wander the site. Wiston Castle remains the most impressive motte castle in this part of Wales.

Wolf's Castle / Cas Blaidd

> Motte
> Location: 7 miles north of Haverfordwest (SM 957 265)
> Access: Visible from the A40

CHECK: To reach the motte and bailey site, head into the village of Wolfscastle, and drive under the overpass carrying the A40. The motte is on the left; the bailey expands to the right.

A good map helps locate the motte castle in Wolfscastle, which is situated immediately alongside the A40 (on its eastern side) between Haverfordwest and Fishguard at the northern end of Treffgarne Gorge and the southern end of the village of Wolf's Castle. Today, the tree and bracken-covered mound is inaccessible, fenced off from human contact alongside a lane leading eastward from the main road, but it is still visible.

Situated on the landward side of a steep promontory, the motte rises some 6 metres high and measures 15.2 metres across the summit. Traces of the oval bailey survive at the site on the south and east sides of the mound; portions along the western side were destroyed when the A40 was built in the late 1920s. Great quantities of medieval and later pottery sherds were discovered in the bailey itself, to the east of a short crescent-shaped earthwork located on the north-eastern side of the motte. That such few artefacts were identified in the lighter coloured soil on the opposite side of the earthwork (closest to the motte) may indicate that the earthwork had actually been part of an Iron Age fort which was largely obliterated when the motte was constructed.

First mentioned in a mandate of 1229 to the Earl Marshal, custodian of the bishopric of St Davids, which granted tenancy of the 'land called *Castrum Lupi*' to Hamo Crassus (Grasse or Grace), the property was considered 'of the fee of the bishopric in the bailiwick of the King [Henry III]'. About 100 years later, four pages of the *Black Book of St Davids* were devoted to discussion of the castle and manor of *Castrum Lupi*. Later references to 'Moldiscastel' probably equates to 'Wolfiscastel', one of several errors made when the 14th-century document was transcribed in the 16th century.

References

Chapter 1
1. *Pembrokeshire County History, volume II: Medieval Pembrokeshire*, edited by R.F. Walker, Pembrokeshire Historical Society

Chapter II
1. *The Lord Rhys, Prince of Deheubarth* by Roger Turvey, (1997), Gomer, p.57
2. *Ibid*, pp.41, 49, 58
3. *Pembrokeshire County History, volume II: Medieval Pembrokeshire*, edited by R.F. Walker, Pembrokeshire Historical Society, pp.201-206

Also from Logaston Press

Pubs of Narberth, Saundersfoot and South-East Pembrokeshire
by Keith Johnson

All existing hostelries in Narberth, Saundersfoot and South-East Pembrokeshire are included, along with many that have come and gone. The first chapters cover the use of south Pembrokeshire coal in the wider brewing industry, and changes in drinking habits and licensing laws over the years. Following chapters each then take a geographical area, with tales of pubs, the reasons behind some of their names, of landlords and of goings on, in which much history of the Narberth wine merchants James Williams is recounted.

There are many 'Chemist's' pubs recorded in the latter half of the 19th century in the area, whereby a chemist who needed a spirit licence to sell certain patent medicines was able to use the same licence to run a pub in the same building! Over the years the licensing authorities gradually insisted that the activities were physically separated by a solid wall. One pub tried to screen its rival from view, by building a wall in the line of sight from the road. Another landlord, desperate to drum up additional business tried topless barmaids. Whilst this generated publicity, it also created animosity. Then he tried an insurance fraud and had the pub burnt down whilst he was on holiday overseas—only to end up in prison.

Many a landlord has developed the accommodation side of their business. However, one visitor found flitches of bacon suspended over his bed, whilst the walls sprouted petticoats, stays, breeches and old wigs; behind the door was a dead pig. When he recounted his tale to others, he was told that it sounded like a perfectly respectable village inn. Fortunately for subsequent visitors the book also tells of many a warm and friendly welcome.

ISBN 1 904396 21 6

Paperback 208 pages with 180 photographs and other illustrations
£9.95

Also from Logaston Press

The Pubs of Pembroke, Pembroke Dock, Tenby and South Pembrokshire
by Keith Johnson

This book details the history and social background of the hotels, taverns and inns that have existed in the area. The first chapters cover the changes in drinking habits and licensing laws over the years, after which a series of chapters each take a geographical area, with tales of pubs, the reasons behind some of their names, of landlords and of goings on. There are stories of poachers, of smugglers (some even renting the ruins of Manorbier Castle to use as a storehouse!), of someone who was so far gone that he felt he could shake hands with a dancing bear, of up market coaching inns and of others where the pigs had to be turned out of the parlour so that customers could sit down.

As early as the end of the 1700s, troopers of the Castlemartin Yeomanry in Pembroke were reputedly so drunk that several slid off their horses on parade, with the kettle drummer playing his instrument with his head. In Pembroke Dock the fortunes of pubs varied with the vicissitudes affecting the dockyard, whilst several were lost in the Second World War bombing. In the meantime, a number were frequented by 'certain kinds of women', to the extent that the service of alcohol seemed to be a secondary business—one pub was even described as a waiting room for the primary activity of a nearby establishment. In contrast, Tenby played host to a strong anti drink movement in the late 19th and early 20th centuries, reducing the numbers of licensed premises to just 20 by 1926, and some of these were out and out hotels. Nevertheless, at one hotel the drinkers faced a 45 yard walk to the toilets in the stables—needless to say, not all ventured that far.

ISBN 1 904396 07 0
Paperback 256 pages with 100 black and white photographs
£9.95